# TED KENNEDY

OKAY, GATHER 'ROUND NOW. THAT'S RIGHT, COME TOGETHER.

HI, FOLKS! MY NAME IS BRENT SPRECHER AND I AM A PAGE WITH THE UNITED STATES SENATE.
I HAVE A SPECIAL TREAT FOR YOU TODAY, AN ALL-ACCESS TOUR OF THE U.S. SENATE BUILDING, WITH VALUABLE INSIGHT INTO THE LIFE AND CAREER OF SENATOR EDWARD "TED" KENNEDY.

TED'S FATHER, JOSEPH P. KENNEDY, GREW THE FAMILY'S FORTUNE AS A FILM MOGUL...

...AND WITH SPECULATIVE INVESTMENT DURING PROHIBITION.

LOANS

BOX

"KENNEDY POLITICS" BEGAN WHEN JOE, A BIG SUPPORTER OF FDR'S PRESIDENTIAL BID, WAS APPOINTED CHIEF OF THE SECURITIES AND EXCHANGE COMMISSION IN 1934.

YOUNG TED LIKED TO READ, BUT HE WAS ALSO QUITE GREGARIOUS AND SOMETHING OF A PERFORMER.

TED WAS ALSO QUITE ATHLETIC, LIKELY DUE TO THE NECESSITY OF HAVING TO KEEP UP WITH HIS MUCH-OLDER, ADVENTUROUS BROTHERS, WHO WERE FOND OF SKIING...

...ROCK-CLIMBING...

...AND SPORTS.

THE KENNEDY CLAN MOVED FREQUENTLY-- BOSTON, NEW YORK, PALM BEACH, LONDON--SO TED BOUNCED FROM ONE PRIVATE SCHOOL TO THE NEXT, ATTENDING TEN SCHOOLS BY THE TIME HE WAS 11 YEARS OLD.

TED DID NOT EXCELL AS A STUDENT...

I DON'T WANT ANY LOSERS IN THIS FAMILY.

...AND WAS A CONSTANT SOURCE OF EMBARRASSMENT TO HIS FAMILY.

HE'S NOTHING LIKE JOE AND JACK. THE BOY IS FAILING HALF OF HIS CLASSES.

THE ONE PLACE WHERE TED DID FIND SUCCESS WAS THE ATHLETIC FIELD.

HOME 0   VISITOR 0

SCHOOL

COACH

UPON GRADUATION FROM THE MILTON ACADEMY, TED FOLLOWED IN HIS BROTHERS' FOOTSTEPS AND ENROLLED AT HARVARD.

UNFORTUNATELY, TED'S SCHOOLING TOOK A BACK SEAT TO HIS LEISURE ACTIVITIES.

TED WAS EXPELLED FROM HARVARD FOR ALLOWING A FRIEND TO TAKE HIS SPANISH FINAL FOR HIM.

OUSTED FROM HARVARD, TED WAS LIKE A SHIP WITHOUT A RUDDER.

HE ENLISTED IN THE ARMY AND HIS FATHER'S POLITICAL INFLUENCE SAW HIM STATIONED IN EUROPE, RATHER THAN IN KOREA, WHERE THE WAR WAS RAGING.

TED WAS READMITTED TO HARVARD FOLLOWING HIS RETURN FROM EUROPE...

...AND ONCE AGAIN TOOK TO SPORTS.

HE WAS EVEN SCOUTED BY THE GREEN BAY PACKERS.

TED TOLD THE PACKERS THAT HE WAS INTERESTED IN ANOTHER "CONTACT SPORT," AND ENROLLED IN LAW SCHOOL FOLLOWING HIS GRADUATION FROM HARVARD.

BY 1954, BOTH ROBERT AND JOHN F. KENNEDY WERE WORKING IN THE POLITICAL ARENA AND TED, A FRESHMAN AT THE UNIVERSITY OF VIRGINIA LAW SCHOOL, WAS ON A FAST TRACK TO FOLLOW THEM.

WHEN ARE WE GOING TO SEE THE SENATE BUILDING?

YEAH!

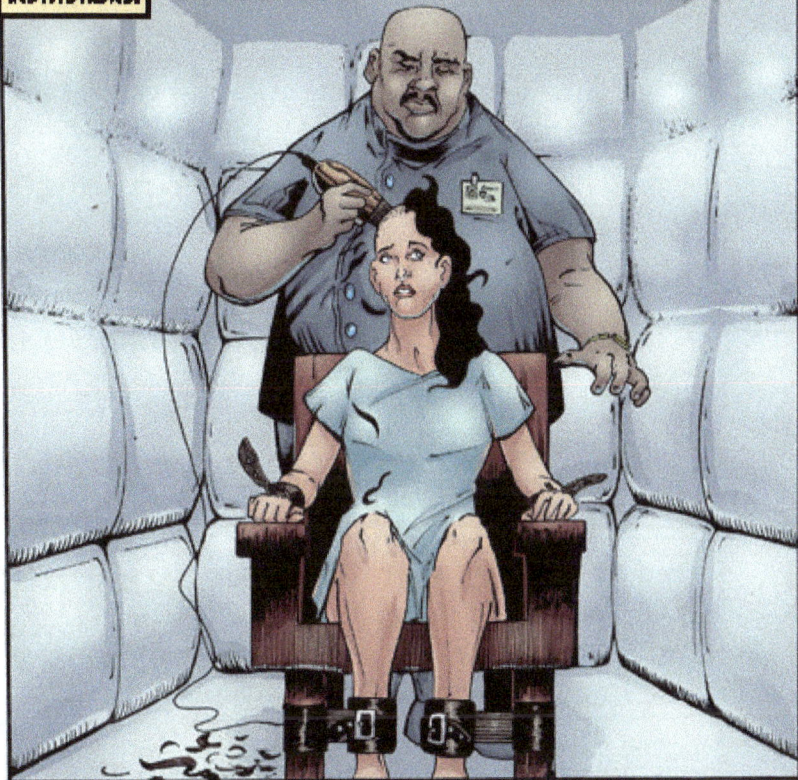

TED'S OLDEST BROTHER, JOE JR., WAS KILLED IN ACTION DURING A RISKY VOLUNTEER MISSION.

KATHLEEN, THE SECOND-OLDEST KENNEDY DAUGHTER, DIED A FEW YEARS LATER IN A PLANE CRASH.

TED'S BROTHERS, JOHN AND ROBERT, FOLLOWED THEIR FATHER INTO POLITICS...

...AND BOTH WERE TAKEN BEFORE THEIR TIME BY ASSASSINS.

TED WAS ALMOST A SHOE-IN TO RUN FOR A PRESIDENTIAL NOMINATION UNTIL A FATEFUL PARTY ON CHAPPAQUIDDICK ISLAND IN 1969.

TED WAS GIVING A RIDE TO MARY JO KOPECHNE, ONE OF THE "BOILER ROOM GIRLS" WHO WORKED FOR HIS BROTHER, ROBERT, WHEN...

...SOMETHING WENT WRONG. TED LOST CONTROL AND THE CAR PLUNGED INTO POUCHA POND.

TED SURVIVED, BUT MARY JO DID NOT. TED LEFT THE SCENE AND FAILED TO REPORT THE ACCIDENT UNTIL THE NEXT DAY.

THE RESULTING SCANDAL RUINED HIS CHANCES OF WINNING THE DEMOCRATIC NOMINATION FOR PRESIDENT IN 1972.

DESPITE THE POLITICAL SET-BACKS AND PERSONAL ATTACKS, SENATOR KENNEDY CONTINUED TO FIGHT FOR THE PEOPLE.

FRANKLY, I DON'T MIND NOT BEING PRESIDENT. JUST MIND THAT SOMEONE ELSE IS.

.IN 1972, KENNEDY BOLSTERED THE *MEALS ON WHEELS* PROGRAM THAT PROVIDES NUTRITIONAL MEALS TO HOMEBOUND SENIOR CITIZENS.

THAT SAME YEAR, KENNEDY THREW HIS SUPPORT BEHIND THE *WIC* BILL TO CREATE A FEDERAL ASSISTANCE PROGRAM FOR LOW-INCOME WOMEN AND THEIR CHILDREN.

KENNEDY BECAME STRONGLY ASSOCIATED WITH THE ISSUES OF GUN CONTROL AND NATIONAL HEALTH INSURANCE IN THE 70'S.

.KENNEDY HAS SPENT HIS ENTIRE CAREER INTRODUCING AND SUPPORTING BILLS AIMED AT AIDING THE DISABLED...

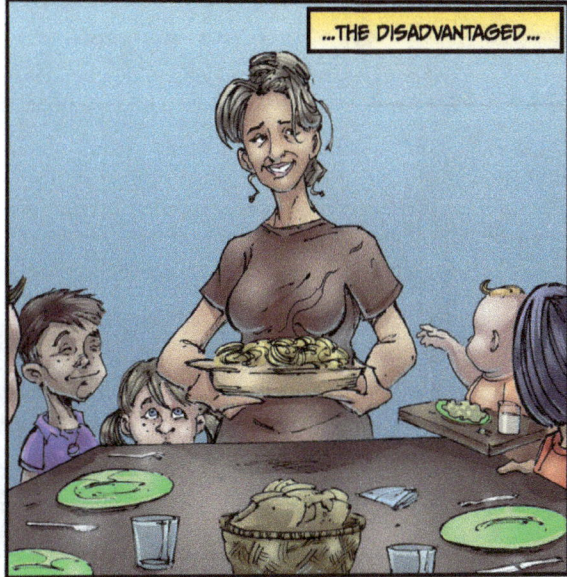

HE CO-SPONSORED THE *CIVIL RIGHTS COMMISSION ACT AMENDMENTS OF 1978*, AIMED AT PREVENTING DISCRIMINATION BASED UPON DISABILITY.

...THE DISADVANTAGED...

...AND THE DISENFRANCHISED.

BUT, KENNEDY'S DON'T RUN FROM CONTROVERSY, THEY CONFRONT IT.

I RECOGNIZE MY OWN SHORTCOMINGS — THE FAULTS IN THE CONDUCT OF MY PRIVATE LIFE. I REALIZE THAT I ALONE AM RESPONSIBLE FOR THEM, AND I AM THE ONE WHO MUST CONFRONT THEM.

DESPITE THE TRAVAILS OF HIS PUBLIC LIFE, TED HAS REMAINED A TIRELESS DEFENDER OF THE PEOPLE.

HE INTRODUCED THE *AMERICANS WITH DISABILITIES ACT* AND THE *RYAN WHITE CARE ACT.*

KENNEDY'S LEADERSHIP DURING THE CLINTON ADMINISTRATION RESULTED IN THE PASSAGE OF SEVERAL ACTS AIMED AT PROVIDING AID TO WORKING FAMILIES.

KENNEDY HAS ALSO SOUGHT BIPARTISAN SUPPORT FOR SUCH IMPORTANT ISSUES AS THE *NO CHILD LEFT BEHIND ACT...*

...AND THE PROTECTION OF OUR TROOPS IN IRAQ.

THE YOUNGEST OF JOE KENNEDY'S CHILDREN IS NOW THE PATRIARCH OF THE FAMILY AND THE KEEPER OF THE KENNEDY FLAME OF PUBLIC SERVICE.

ONE PERSON CAN MAKE A DIFFERENCE AND EVERY ONE SHOULD TRY.

TED'S WIFE, VICTORIA REGGIE KENNEDY, HAS HELPED HIM CAMPAIGN AND IS A VERY ACTIVE ADVOCATE FOR GUN SAFETY.

Gun Control Association

TED'S SON, PATRICK, BECAME THE YOUNGEST KENNEDY TO HOLD PUBLIC OFFICE WHEN HE WON ELECTION TO THE RHODE ISLAND STATE ASSEMBLY AT THE AGE OF 21.

PATRICK CONTINUES TO SERVE AND, LIKE HIS FATHER, HAS MADE HEALTH CARE ONE OF HIS KEY CONCERNS.

VOTE FOR CHANGE

OBAMA

VOTE

STAND FOR CHANGE

VOTE

TED KENNEDY IS ONE OF THE NATION'S MOST INFLUENTIAL POLITICIANS AND HAS OFTEN BEEN REFERRED TO AS A "DEMOCRATIC ICON."

HIS EARLY SUPPORT OF BARACK OBAMA HELPED THE ILLINOIS SENATOR GAIN THE DEMOCRATIC PARTY NOMINATION FOR THE PRESIDENCY.

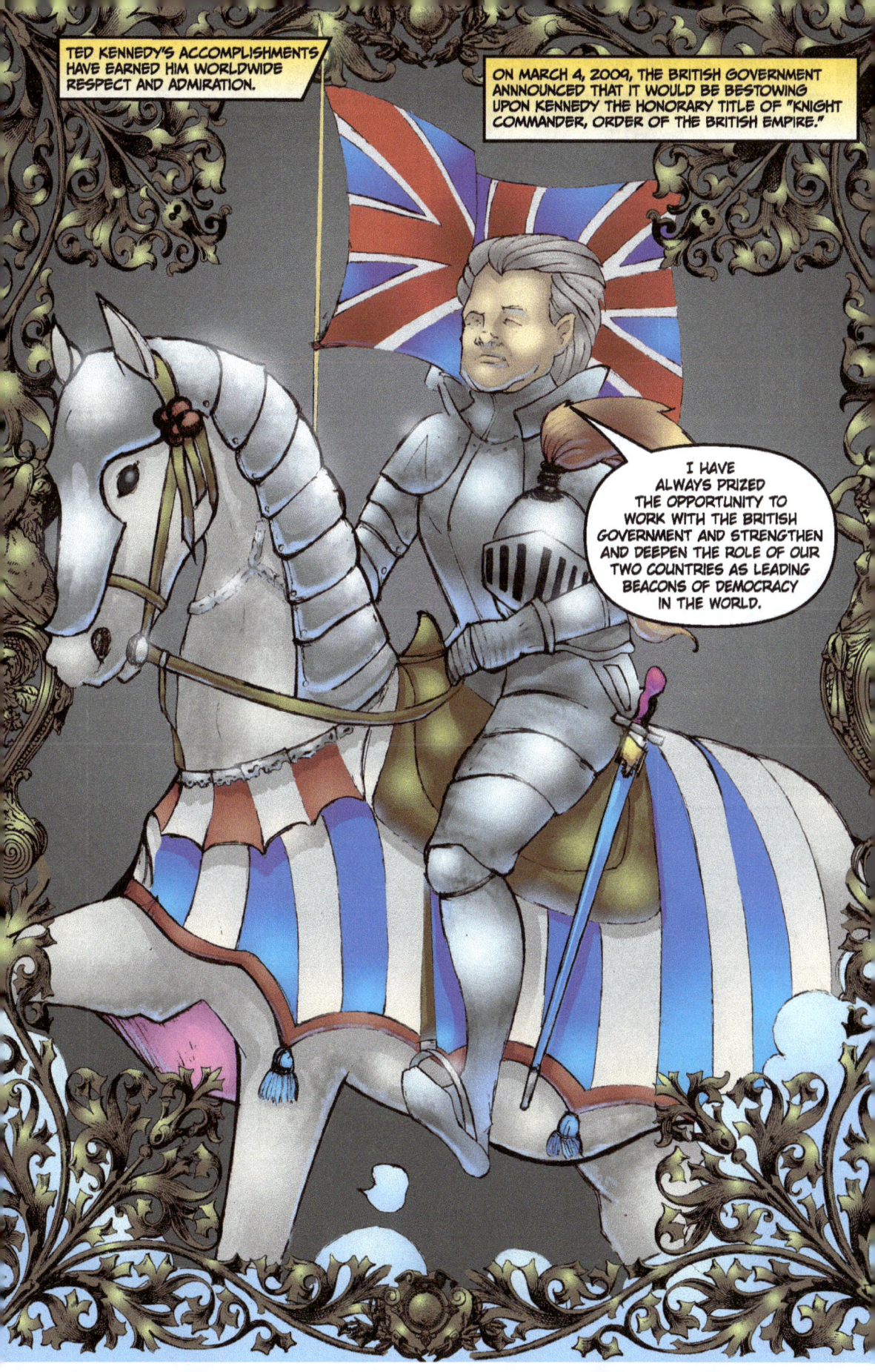

NOW IN HIS LATE 70'S, KENNEDY HAS BEEN STRUGGLING WITH HEALTH ISSUES FOR YEARS. AFTER SUFFERING TWO SEIZURES LAST YEAR, TED WAS DIAGNOSED WITH A CANCEROUS BRAIN TUMOR.

TED'S CONDITION REQUIRED SURGERY AND HE SPENT SEVERAL MONTHS RECUPERATING IN FLORIDA.

STILL QUITE ILL, HE MANAGED TO ATTEND THE FIRST NIGHT OF THE DEMOCRATIC NATIONAL CONVENTION IN AUGUST 2008, WHERE HE WAS HONORED IN A SPECIAL PRESENTATION.

KENNEDY SEEMED SPRY AT A STAR-STUDDED BIRTHDAY CONCERT HELD FOR HIM AT THE KENNEDY CENTER...

...AND HE EVEN THREW A PITCH WITH SOME "HEAT" TO OPEN THE RED SOX'S 2009 BASEBALL SEASON.

EIGHTEEN
MILLION VOTES.

TOTAL US POPULATION,
306 MILLION (APPX).

THAT'S THE ENTIRE POPULATION
OF NEW MEXICO, WEST VIRGINIA,
NEBRASKA, IDAHO, MAINE, NEW
HAMPSHIRE, HAWAII, RHODE
ISLAND, MONTANA, DELAWARE,
NORTH AND SOUTH DAKOTA,
ALASKA, WYOMING, VERMONT,
AND THE DISTRICT OF COLUMBIA.

NOT THE VOTING
POPULATION;
*EVERYBODY IN
THE STATE.*

IT'S ALSO THE ENTIRE
POPULATION OF WEST
VIRGINIA, NEW MEXICO,
UTAH, KANSAS,
ARKANSAS, AND
MISSISSIPPI.

IT'S THE ENTIRE POPULATION
OF IOWA, CONNECTICUT,
OKLAHOMA, OREGON, AND
PUERTO RICO...

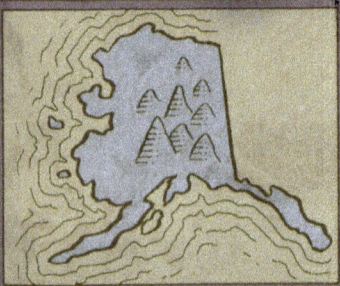

...IT'S ALSO KENTUCKY, LOUISIANA, SOUTH CAROLINA, AND ALABAMA COMBINED.

IT'S ALMOST EVERY SINGLE PERSON IN THE STATE OF NEW YORK.

THAT'S HOW MANY PEOPLE VOTED FOR HILLARY CLINTON IN THE DEMOCRATIC PRIMARIES, TO SAY NOTHING OF HOW SHE MIGHT HAVE FARED IN A GENERAL ELECTION.

TO PUT THIS IN PERSPECTIVE, IN 1988 LENORA FULANI RECEIVED APPROXIMATELY 217,000 VOTES FOR PRESIDENT, TO DATE THE CLOSEST WOMAN TO THE PRESIDENCY OF THE UNITED STATES.

THINK WHAT YOU WILL ABOUT HILLARY CLINTON; HER LIFE IS HISTORIC, AND HER ACHIEVEMENT IN THIS LAST ELECTION, BOTH FOR WOMEN AND FOR EQUALITY, IS MONUMENTAL.

HEY. I'M NEAL, THE LOWLY WRITER. COMING INTO THIS PROJECT, I HAD APPREHENSIONS. I MEAN, IT'S HILLARY CLINTON! SHE TRIED TO BAN GRAND THEFT AUTO, RIGHT? MY EDITOR APPROACHED ME FOR THIS AND I *BALKED.*

BUT RESEARCHING I REALIZED, THE NUMBERS AND THE HISTORY MAKE IT IMPOSSIBLE *NOT* TO ADMIRE HILLARY'S ACHIEVEMENT. SO TO THE SKEPTICS I SAY, GIVE THIS A CHANCE.

I WRITE THIS OUT OF RESPECT FOR THE WOMAN. I DO IT, HOPEFULLY, WITH A CLEAR AND HONEST PERSPECTIVE. I WILL NOT HIDE HER WARTS, AS THEY ARE PART OF HOW WE REGARD HER.

I BELIEVE SHE SPOKE TO HER OWN ACCOMPLISHMENT WELL WHEN SHE SUSPENDED HER CAMPAIGN ON JUNE 7, 2008:

THERE ARE NO ACCEPTABLE LIMITS, AND THERE ARE NO ACCEPTABLE PREJUDICES IN THE 21ST CENTURY IN OUR COUNTRY.

YOU CAN BE SO PROUD THAT FROM NOW ON, IT WILL BE *UN*REMARKABLE FOR A WOMAN TO WIN PRIMARY STATE VICTORIES,

*UN*REMARKABLE TO HAVE A WOMAN IN A CLOSE RACE TO BE OUR NOMINEE,

*UN*REMARKABLE TO THINK THAT A WOMAN CAN BE THE PRESIDENT OF THE UNITED STATES,

AND *THAT* IS TRULY REMARKABLE.

SHE WAS BORN IN CHICAGO IN 1947 TO A FATHER IN THE TEXTILE INDUSTRY AND A STAY-AT-HOME MOTHER.

SUBURBAN PARK RIDGE PUBLIC ELEMENTARY SCHOOLS PROVIDED EDUCATION, WHERE SHE EXCELLED. SHE JOINED THE GIRL SCOUTS, FIRST AS A BROWNIE, THEN A FULL-FLEDGED SCOUT.

FROM EARLY ON, SHE WAS INTERESTED IN POLITICS, INVOLVING HERSELF IN STUDENT GOVERNMENT, SPORTS, AND CHURCH ACTIVITIES.

SHE GREW UP HERE, IN A HOUSE HOWARD ROARK MIGHT HAVE RESENTED FOR ITS BLOCKINESS, ADOPTING HER FAMILY'S VALUES AND GROWING ENAMORED OF GOD AND COUNTRY.

IT MIGHT SURPRISE YOU TO LEARN SHE THEN BECAME A REPUBLICAN, GIVEN HER HISTORY AS A DEMOCRAT.

SHE WORKED FOR THE GOLDWATER CAMPAIGN IN 1964 WHEN SHE WAS JUST A TEENAGER.

HE LOST TO LYNDON JOHNSON, BUT SHE REMAINED A REPUBLICAN, EVEN INTO HER COLLEGE YEARS.

IN THE WAKE OF THE NUCLEAR AGE, SURROUNDED BY THE CHAOS OF THE VIETNAM WAR, THE ASSASSINATION OF JOHN F. KENNEDY AND HIS BROTHER, ROBERT KENNEDY, AND FACING THE TUMULT OF A NATION AT MORAL WAR WITH ITSELF, HILLARY EXPLORED BOTH MAJOR AMERICAN POLITICAL PHILOSOPHIES.

IN 1962, SHE WATCHED MARTIN LUTHER KING GIVE A SPEECH, A SPEECH THAT THAT GREATLY IMPACTED HER PERSONALLY, PUSHING HER TO PUBLIC SERVICE.

7089

HILLARY CLINTON IDOLIZED MARTIN LUTHER KING AS A MAN WHO FOUGHT FOR WHAT HE BELIEVED IN, A MAN WHO WAS CATEGORICALLY AGAINST THE WAR IN VIETNAM AND FOR RACIAL TOLERANCE. A MAN TORTURED FOR BEING IN THE MINORITY. A MAN OF VISION.

STUDENTS HILLARY'S AGE WERE BEING KILLED ON THE STREETS AS PROTESTS RAGED OVER UNPOPULAR WARS.

ALL AROUND HER VALUES WERE CHANGING AND THE NATION WAS IN TURMOIL. AMERICA LOST HER INNOCENCE IN MANY CRITICAL WAYS.

WAS IT THE ASSASSINATION OF DR. KING? THE POLITICAL UPHEAVAL? MAYBE IT WAS SIMPLE PHILOSOPHY. REGARDLESS, HILLARY CLINTON STARTED A REPUBLICAN, AND THROUGH THE EVENTS SHE WITNESSED AS A NATION RE-DEFINED ITSELF, SHE ENDED A DEMOCRAT.

SHE EARNED RESPECT EARLY ON, BECOMING THE FIRST STUDENT AT WELLESLEY ASKED TO GIVE A COMMENCEMENT ADDRESS. IT WAS EASY TO SEE, READING THE SPEECH FOR RESEARCH, EXACTLY WHY:

AND THEN RESPECT. THERE'S THAT MUTUALITY OF RESPECT BETWEEN PEOPLE WHERE YOU DON'T SEE PEOPLE AS PERCENTAGE POINTS. WHERE YOU DON'T MANIPULATE PEOPLE. WHERE YOU'RE NOT INTERESTED IN SOCIAL ENGINEERING FOR PEOPLE.

THE STRUGGLE FOR AN INTEGRATED LIFE EXISTING IN AN ATMOSPHERE OF COMMUNAL TRUST AND RESPECT IS ONE WITH DESPERATELY IMPORTANT POLITICAL AND SOCIAL CONSEQUENCES. AND THE WORD "CONSEQUENCES" OF COURSE CATAPULTS US INTO THE FUTURE.

ONE OF THE MOST TRAGIC THINGS THAT HAPPENED YESTERDAY, A BEAUTIFUL DAY, WAS THAT I WAS TALKING TO WOMAN WHO SAID THAT SHE WOULDN'T WANT TO BE ME FOR ANYTHING IN THE WORLD. SHE WOULDN'T WANT TO LIVE TODAY AND LOOK AHEAD TO WHAT IT IS SHE SEES BECAUSE SHE'S AFRAID. FEAR IS ALWAYS WITH US BUT WE JUST DON'T HAVE TIME FOR IT. NOT NOW.

SHE RECEIVED A SEVEN MINUTE STANDING OVATION.

READING THAT SCRIPT, ANYONE COULD SEE WHY.

SHE WENT TO YALE AFTER A SUMMER OF SLIMING FISH, A SUMMER IN WHICH SHE NEARLY SHUT DOWN THE CANNERY BY NOTING UNHEALTHY WORKING CONDITIONS.

SHE STUDIED EARLY CHILDHOOD DEVELOPMENT AND WORKED IN THE YALE CHILD STUDY CENTER.

SHE BEGAN DATING A SIGNIFICANTLY HAIRIER BILL CLINTON THAN THE PRESIDENT WE KNOW, AND ALSO BEGAN DEFINING HER SCHOLARLY AMBITION, RELEASING PAPERS ON THE COGNIZANCE OF CHILDREN THAT WERE OFT-CITED AND WELL-REGARDED.

SHE TURNED DOWN BILL'S REQUEST FOR MARRIAGE AT FIRST, ATTENDING TO HER STUDIES AND FOCUSING ON HER CAREER. UNLIKE NOW, THIS WAS HARDLY COMMONPLACE, AND A DECISION THAT FAMILY SPURNED.

WHEN THEY EVENTUALLY MARRIED, SHE KEPT HER MAIDEN NAME, RODHAM, MUCH TO THE CHAGRIN OF BOTH THE MOTHER OF THE BRIDE AND THE MOTHER OF THE GROOM.

SHE WAS ONE OF TWO FEMALE LAWYERS SERVING ON THE HOUSE JUDICIARY COMMITTEE THAT RESEARCHED THE POTENTIALITY OF IMPEACHMENT FOR RICHARD NIXON BEFORE HE RESIGNED.

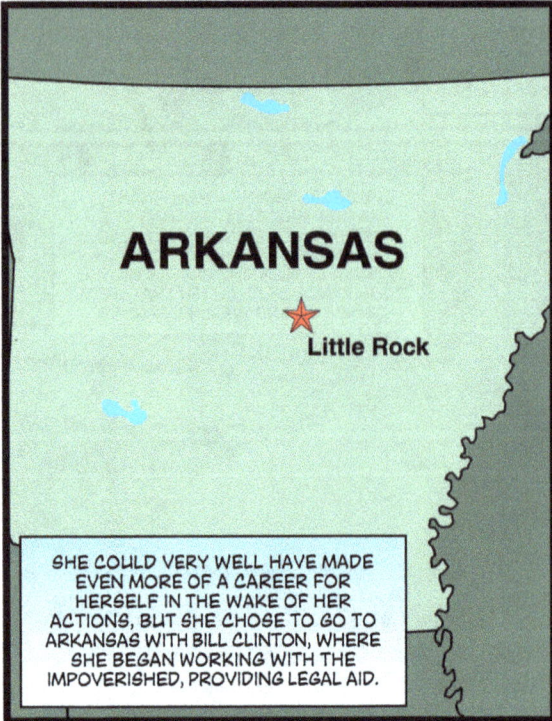

**ARKANSAS**

★ Little Rock

SHE COULD VERY WELL HAVE MADE EVEN MORE OF A CAREER FOR HERSELF IN THE WAKE OF HER ACTIONS, BUT SHE CHOSE TO GO TO ARKANSAS WITH BILL CLINTON, WHERE SHE BEGAN WORKING WITH THE IMPOVERISHED, PROVIDING LEGAL AID.

WHILE HER HUSBAND RECEIVED AN EXTRAORDINARY AMOUNT OF MEDIA ATTENTION, ACHIEVING SUCCESS IN HIS BID FOR THE GOVERNOR OF ARKANSAS, HILLARY EARNED SUCCESS OF HER OWN, BECOMING THE FIRST FEMALE PARTNER OF THE ROSE LAW FIRM, WHERE SHE WORKED QUIETLY FROM 1980 TO 1992.

ARKANSAS ADVOCATES FOR CHILDREN & FAMILIES

DURING THIS TIME SHE FOUNDED THE ARKANSAS ADVOCATES FOR CHILDREN AND FAMILIES, A LEGAL AID ADVOCACY GROUP, AND FOUGHT TO SAVE IT FROM BUDGET CUTS AS REAGAN TRIED TO TRIM THE BUDGET.

MUCH HAS BEEN MADE OF THE YEARS BETWEEN 1980 AND 1992 BY THE MEDIA, GIVEN THAT HILLARY WAS NOT AS MUCH IN THE PUBLIC SPOTLIGHT...

SPECULATION GREW, IN RETROSPECT, WHEN BILL CLINTON ACHIEVED THE PRESIDENCY.

A THOUSAND DOLLAR INVESTMENT BECAME A HUNDRED THOUSAND DOLLAR PROFIT IN CATTLE FUTURES, AND PEOPLE SAW SCANDAL.

THERE CAME OTHER ALLEGATIONS THAT SHE AND HER HUSBAND ENGAGED IN WRONGDOING BY PURCHASING PLOTS OF LAND TO SUBDIVIDE AND SELL. WHITEWATER.

ULTIMATELY, THESE TURNED OUT TO BE LEGALLY BASELESS ACCUSATIONS IN A PERIOD OF HISTORY WHERE CONTROVERSY WAS LESS DEFINED THAN IT IS NOW. JUST LOOK AROUND.

IRONICALLY, A WOMAN BIRTHED IN TIMES OF TRUE CHAOS BECAME A PARIAH IN AN ERA OF CHANGE HER FAMILY HAD HELPED USHER IN. SHE EVEN GAVE THE PRESS CONFERENCE, INITIALLY, TO QUIET THE PRESS, IN PLACE OF HER HUSBAND.

SHE WAS TREATED AS A FULL PARTNER IN THE PRESIDENCY.

MAYBE THIS IRKED A MAN LIKE KEN STARR. MAYBE HE REALLY SOUGHT JUSTICE

THE REALITY OF HER SCANDALS?

SHE WAS WORKING TO MAKE HER NAME IN LAW AND RAISING HER DAUGHTER CHELSEA, WHO WAS BORN IN 1980. I'M OLDER BY A FEW MONTHS.

THAT'S SAD.

YOUR HUMBLE AUTHOR IS OLD.

THE CLINTON PRESIDENCY, WHETHER YOU AGREE WITH THE ALLEGATIONS OR NOT, WAS MARKED WITH CONTROVERSY.

EVEN AS THINGS SEEMED AT THEIR BRIGHTEST IN TERMS OF HOPE FOR THE COUPLE, SORDID NEWS STORIES EMERGED IN TABLOIDS. STORIES WITH BASIS IN FACT.

BILL CLINTON HAD AN AFFAIR WITH A WOMAN NAMED GENNIFER FLOWERS, AN AFFAIR DENIED BY THE COUPLE AT THE TIME.

SHE WAS TERRIFIED. YOU KNOW, AN AVERAGE PERSON IS NOT-

BILL AND HILLARY SPOKE WITH 60 MINUTES IN AN ATTEMPT TO RECTIFY THE PUBLIC PERCEPTION OF INFIDELITY.

JESUS MARY AND JOSEPH!

THE INTERVIEW WENT WELL, EVEN IF A STAGE LIGHT TRIED TO KILL THE FUTURE FIRST LADY.

IT'S CREDITED WITH SAVING BILL'S POSITION IN THE RACE, EVEN IF HE LATER ADMITTED TO AN AFFAIR. WHETHER HILLARY KNEW OF THE AFFAIR AT THE TIME IS OF YET UNCLEAR.

REGARDLESS, CLINTON WON THE ELECTION AND BEGAN A PERIOD OF PROSPERITY DESPITE THE CONTROVERSIES THAT WOULD SWIRL AROUND HIS OFFICE OVER SEXUAL ALLEGATIONS.

AS THE ONLY WEALTHY NATION IN THE MODERN WORLD WITHOUT UNIVERSAL HEALTH CARE, THE UNITED STATES IS AT WAR WITH ITSELF OVER HOW TO HANDLE ITS TEEMING MASSES OF SICK.

HILLARY SOUGHT TO GET UNIVERSAL HEALTH CARE IN THE UNITED STATES, GIVING TESTIMONY BEFORE CONGRESS AND HOLDING CONTROVERSIAL CLOSED-DOOR MEETINGS IN AN ATTEMPT TO BRING HER ISSUE TO BEAR.

SHE WAS MOCKED AND DERIDED, HER PLAN CALLED "HILLARYCARE," AND HER POLITICAL CAPITAL LESSENED. THE OUTSIDE PERSPECTIVE WAS THAT SHE WAS TAKING OFFICE WITHOUT HAVING EARNED IT, AND HER PUBLIC OPINION SUFFERED DESPITE OBVIOUS GOOD INTENTIONS.

SHE SUFFERED UNDER THE PUBLIC MISPERCEPTION OF HER LACK OF QUALIFICATION, SEEING AS BEFORE HER, NO FIRST LADY HAD EVER HAD A PROFESSIONAL CAREER BEFORE THE WHITE HOUSE.

THIS PLAN, COUPLED WITH THE ALLEGATIONS OF CORRUPTION, LED TO THE REPUBLICANS TAKING THE HOUSE OF REPRESENTATIVES FOR THE FIRST TIME SINCE 1954.

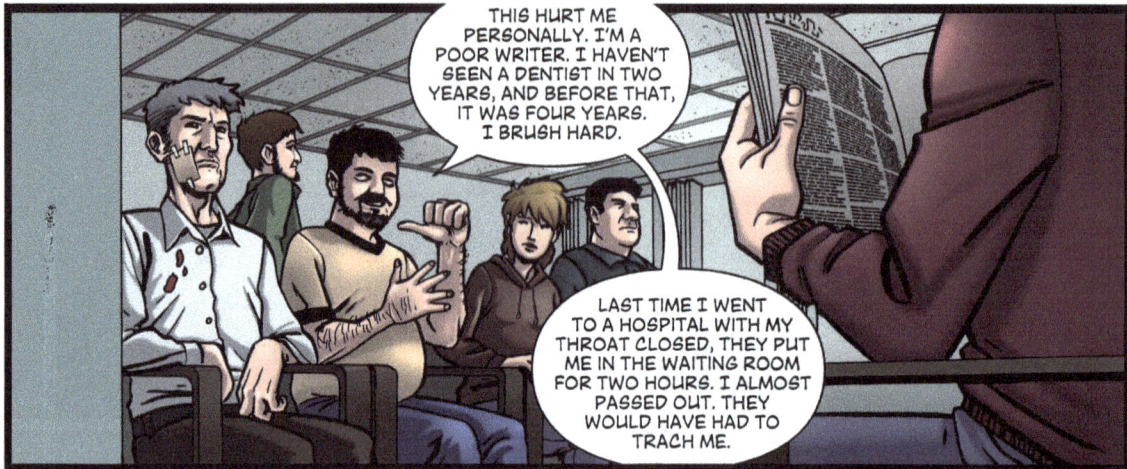

AS MUCH AS BILL CLINTON HAS DONE FOR THIS COUNTRY, HIS PRESIDENCY WAS MARRED WITH SCANDALS OF INFIDELITY. THEY UNDERMINED HIS GOOD WORKS IN THE EYES OF MANY AT THE TIME.

IN 1998, THE PRESS, NOTABLY THE DRUDGE REPORT, POUNCED ON THE LEWINSKY SCANDAL, CAUSING THE PRESIDENT TO DECLARE, WITH VEHEMENCE:

I DID... NOT... HAVE... SEXUAL... RELATIONS... WITH... THAT... WOMAN!

BUT HE HAD. HE WAS BROUGHT UP ON PERJURY CHARGES AND PUBLICLY CENSURED.

DESPITE LEAVING OFFICE WITH THE HIGHEST APPROVAL RATING OF ANY PRESIDENT IN POLL HISTORY, HE LEFT IN A WASH OF SCANDAL.

NO BIOGRAPHY I COULD FIND MENTIONS HILLARY'S REACTION TO THIS. NOTHING COVERS THE EMOTIONAL DAMAGE IT MUST HAVE CAUSED. HER GRIEF IN THIS MATTER IS LOST TO HISTORY.

BUT IT MUST BE CONSIDERABLE. IT MADE HER, FOR ONCE, RASH.

THE GREAT STORY HERE FOR ANYBODY WILLING TO FIND IT AND WRITE ABOUT IT AND EXPLAIN IT IS THIS VAST RIGHT-WING CONSPIRACY THAT HAS BEEN CONSPIRING AGAINST MY HUSBAND SINCE THE DAY HE ANNOUNCED FOR PRESIDENT.

SHE CRACKED ONCE IN A MOMENT OF TRUE PRESSURE, AND THE MEDIA ASSAILED HER FOR IT. TEN YEARS LATER, THEY STILL JOKE ABOUT THE "RIGHT-WING CONSPIRACY" COMMENT, FOR AS LITTLE AS IT TRULY MEANT AT THE TIME.

UNDAUNTED, HILLARY SPRUNG BACK IN THE WAKE OF THE SCANDAL AND RAN FOR PUBLIC OFFICE ON HER OWN AS A SENATOR FOR THE STATE OF NEW YORK.

SHE WON, AND HAS MAINTAINED HER SENATE SEAT SINCE 2000.

THE FIRST FIRST LADY EVER TO RUN FOR PUBLIC OFFICE.

THE FIRST FIRST LADY WITH A POST-BACCALAUREATE DEGREE.

THE FIRST FIRST LADY WITH AN OFFICE IN THE WEST WING.

AND AS MENTIONED, THE FIRST FIRST LADY TO HAVE A PROFESSIONAL CAREER BEFORE THE WHITE HOUSE.

MANY, MANY FIRSTS. THERE ISN'T ENOUGH ROOM HERE FOR THEM ALL.

BUT 9/11 CHANGED EVERYTHING!

YES. IT DID.

WITCHHUNTS BEGAN. WE FOUNDED A DEPARTMENT OF HOMELAND SECURITY, WHICH, BEFORE 9/11, WOULD SOUND IN NAME ALONE LIKE SOME CRAZY ORWELLIAN CRACKPOT SCHEME.

Maher

THERE WERE EVEN LISTS OF SONGS THAT CONGLOMERATES ASKED NOT BE PLAYED ON THE RADIO. YOU KNOW, SO WE WOULDN'T LET THE TERRORISTS CHANGE OUR WAY OF LIFE.

IT LED FRIGHTENED SENATORS TO SIGN THE USA P.A.T.R.I.O.T. ACT, NOW LONG CRITICIZED FOR ABRIDGING CIVIL RIGHTS OVER ITS INTENT AS AN ANTI-TERRORISM MEASURE.

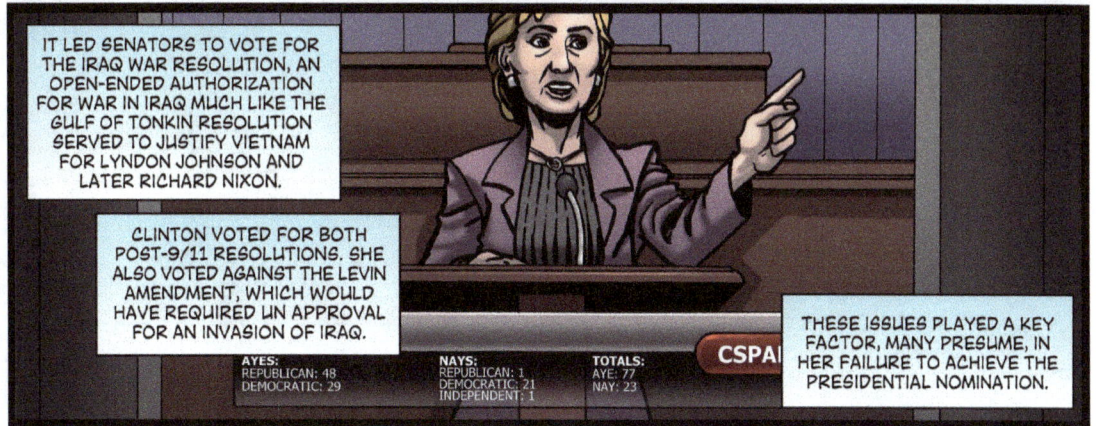

IT LED SENATORS TO VOTE FOR THE IRAQ WAR RESOLUTION, AN OPEN-ENDED AUTHORIZATION FOR WAR IN IRAQ MUCH LIKE THE GULF OF TONKIN RESOLUTION SERVED TO JUSTIFY VIETNAM FOR LYNDON JOHNSON AND LATER RICHARD NIXON.

CLINTON VOTED FOR BOTH POST-9/11 RESOLUTIONS. SHE ALSO VOTED AGAINST THE LEVIN AMENDMENT, WHICH WOULD HAVE REQUIRED UN APPROVAL FOR AN INVASION OF IRAQ.

THESE ISSUES PLAYED A KEY FACTOR, MANY PRESUME, IN HER FAILURE TO ACHIEVE THE PRESIDENTIAL NOMINATION.

CSPAN

| AYES: | NAYS: | TOTALS: |
|---|---|---|
| REPUBLICAN: 48 | REPUBLICAN: 1 | AYE: 77 |
| DEMOCRATIC: 29 | DEMOCRATIC: 21 | NAY: 23 |
| | INDEPENDENT: 1 | |

BUT THAT'S FOCUSING ON ONLY HALF OF HER SENATE CAREER. SHE ALSO FOUGHT FOR RECONSTRUCTION MONEY FOR NEW YORK IN THE WAKE OF THE TERRORIST ATTACKS.

SHE FOUGHT AGAINST BUSH'S TAX CUTS, WHICH PROVIDED A DISPROPORTIONATE BREAK TO THE WEALTHIEST CITIZENS IN OUR NATION.

SHE WON EASY RE-ELECTION IN 2004 BECAUSE OF IT, AND BECAME AN EASY CANDIDATE FOR PRESIDENCY. PEOPLE HAD BEEN TALKING ABOUT IT SINCE THE CONTROVERSIAL ELECTION OF 2000.

HECK, PEOPLE WERE TALKING ABOUT IT IN 1969.

SHE SOON DECLARED HER CANDIDACY FOR THE 2008 RACE, TO RESOUNDING ENTHUSIASM.

...ONLY A NEW PRESIDENT WILL BE ABLE TO UNDO BUSH'S MISTAKES AND RESTORE OUR HOPE AND OPTIMISM.

ONLY A NEW PRESIDENT CAN RENEW THE PROMISE OF AMERICA. THE IDEA THAT IF YOU WORK HARD YOU CAN COUNT ON THE HEALTH CARE, EDUCATION, AND RETIREMENT SECURITY THAT YOU NEED TO RAISE YOUR FAMILY.

THESE ARE THE BASIC VALUES OF AMERICA THAT ARE UNDER ATTACK FROM THIS ADMINISTRATION EVERY DAY.

HER SUCCESS WAS VIEWED AS INEVITABLE. AMERICA LOVES A DYNASTIC CYCLE IN HER POLITICS, AND AFTER BUSH JR. FOLLOWED BUSH SR., AND WITH A COUNTRY ACHING FOR THE PROSPERITY OF THE CLINTON YEARS, HER NOMINATION SEEMED A FOREGONE CONCLUSION.

PRIMARY VOTES: 126

VS

PRIMARY VOTES: 174

TO WIT, SHE WON THE FIRST TWO PRIMARIES, BUT THESE PRIMARIES WERE STRICKEN FROM THE RECORD FOR BREAKING PARTY RULES IN ORDER TO ENCOURAGE TOURISM AND GAIN MEDIA ATTENTION. IN THE PUBLIC EYE, SHE TOOK AN EARLY LEAD.

THE INEVITABLE RETURN TO BASHING BEGAN, AS IT HAD DURING HER HUSBAND'S PRESIDENCY, ONLY THIS TIME IN AN ARENA WHERE BASHING IS CALLED FOR, EVEN EXPECTED.

ACCUSATIONS FLEW. THE RACE CARD. THE SEX CARD. THE CLINTON CARD.

IF SHE ASKED THEM TO SILENCE MISOGYNIST CRITIQUE, SHE WAS NOT "MAN" ENOUGH TO HANDLE EXECUTIVE OFFICE. IF SHE JUST TOUGHED IT OUT, HER CRITICS RAN UNOPPOSED.

EVEN A MOMENT OF HUMAN EMOTION, WHEN HILLARY BROKE DOWN IN TEARS AT A CAMPAIGN STOP, BECAME A POLITICAL QUESTION FROM A CYNICAL PRESS.

WAS SHE CRYING BECAUSE SHE WAS TRYING TO GET PEOPLE TO VOTE FOR HER? OR WAS SHE BREAKING DOWN BECAUSE SHE WAS AN HONEST HUMAN BEING?

ONE THING PLAIN TO SEE IS THAT BECAUSE OF HER POSITION AS A FIRST LADY, BECAUSE OF HER "FIRSTS," FROM THE BEGINNING SHE'S BEEN DEMONIZED. IS THIS BECAUSE SHE'S A WOMAN? IS IT BECAUSE SHE'S BOLD? IS IT BECAUSE THERE'S SOME JUSTICE TO THE CRITIQUE?

DOES IT EVEN MATTER?

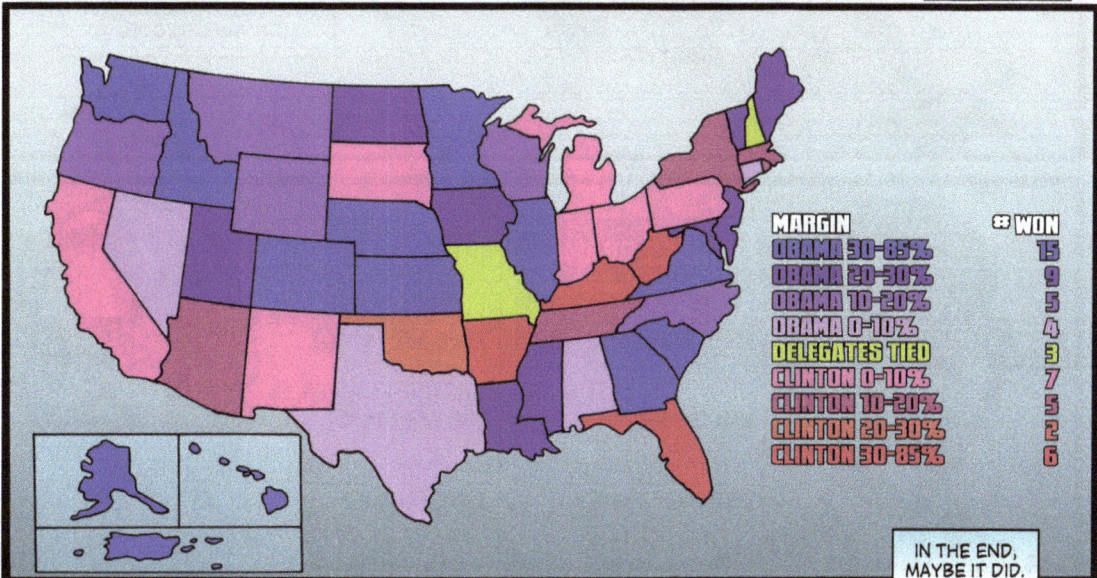

| MARGIN | # WON |
|---|---|
| OBAMA 30-85% | 15 |
| OBAMA 20-30% | 9 |
| OBAMA 10-20% | 5 |
| OBAMA 0-10% | 4 |
| DELEGATES TIED | 3 |
| CLINTON 0-10% | 7 |
| CLINTON 10-20% | 5 |
| CLINTON 20-30% | 2 |
| CLINTON 30-85% | 6 |

IN THE END, MAYBE IT DID.

SLOWLY BUT SURELY, OBAMA TOOK THE LEAD. HE LOST KEY BATTLEGROUND STATES, BUT SUCCEEDED IN MULTIPLE SMALLER ELECTIONS, ULTIMATELY SWINGING PUBLIC FAVOR HIS WAY.

HER FORMER ALLIES BEGAN TO ENCOURAGE HER TO LEAVE THE RACE GIVEN THAT MATHEMATICALLY, IT WAS IMPOSSIBLE BARRING NIXON APPROVAL NUMBERS FROM OBAMA FOR HER TO SUCCEED.

FEARS WERE RAISED THAT SHE WOULD SPLIT THE PARTY AND GIVE MCCAIN THE ELECTION.

OBAMA ☐ HILLARY ☐

TH' HELL?

AYUH.

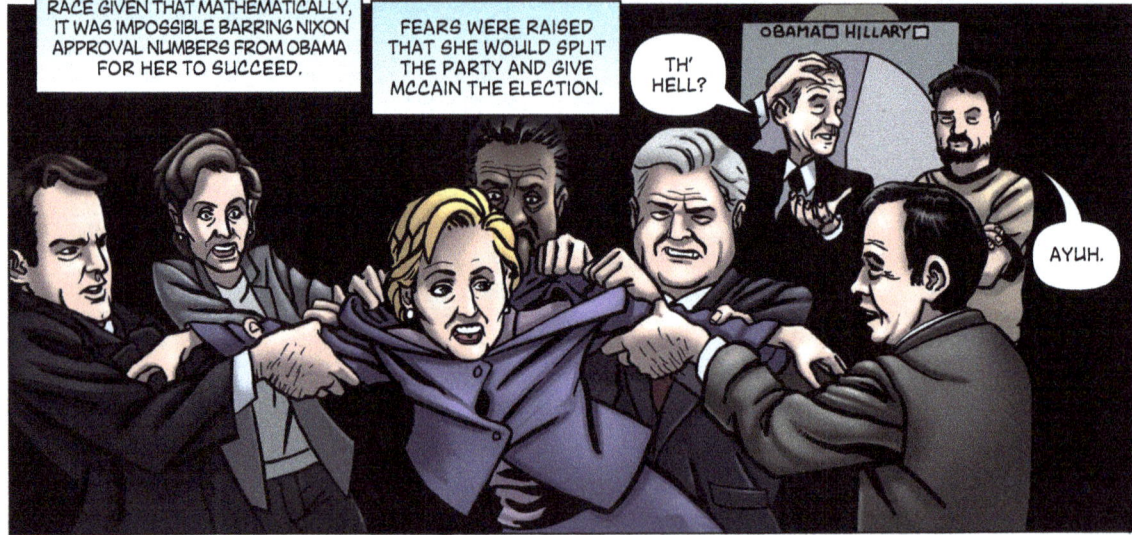

THE FABLED GLASS CEILING? MISOGYNY? INEPTITUDE? STUPIDITY? DEMOCRACY AT WORK? AGAIN, WHO KNOWS?

AS NOTED, HILLARY SUSPENDED HER CAMPAIGN ON JUNE 7, 2008.

| BARACK OBAMA | HILLARY CLINTON |
|---|---|
| PLEDGED DELEGATES: 1,828 1/2 (52%) | PLEDGED DELEGATES: 1,726 1/2 (48%) |
| SUPERDELEGATES: 478 (66%) | SUPERDELEGATES: 246 1/2 (34%) |
| TOTAL DELEGATES: 2,306 1/2 (54%) | TOTAL DELEGATES: 1,973 (46%) |
| WINNER! | |

THIS IS SUBJECTIVE, AND I'M BREAKING IMPARTIALITY, BUT I THINK SHE ACCEPTED GRACEFULLY IN THE WAKE OF HOW HARD SHE FOUGHT. I THOUGHT SHE WOULD NEVER GIVE UP. AND IT TURNS OUT SHE DIDN'T. SHE JUST SHIFTED HER FOCUS.
I AM HONORED TO BE HERE TONIGHT. A PROUD MOTHER. A PROUD DEMOCRAT. A PROUD AMERICAN. AND A PROUD SUPPORTER OF BARACK OBAMA.
MY FRIENDS, IT IS TIME TO TAKE BACK THE COUNTRY WE LOVE.
WHETHER YOU VOTED FOR ME, OR VOTED FOR BARACK, THE TIME IS NOW TO UNITE AS A SINGLE PARTY WITH A SINGLE PURPOSE. WE ARE ON THE SAME TEAM, AND NONE OF US CAN SIT ON THE SIDELINES.
THIS IS A FIGHT FOR THE FUTURE. AND IT'S A FIGHT WE MUST WIN.
I HAVEN'T SPENT THE PAST 35 YEARS IN THE TRENCHES ADVOCATING FOR CHILDREN, CAMPAIGNING FOR UNIVERSAL HEALTH CARE, HELPING PARENTS BALANCE WORK AND FAMILY, AND FIGHTING FOR WOMEN'S RIGHTS AT HOME AND AROUND THE WORLD TO SEE ANOTHER REPUBLICAN IN THE WHITE HOUSE SQUANDER THE PROMISE OF OUR COUNTRY AND THE HOPES OF OUR PEOPLE.
AND YOU HAVEN'T WORKED SO HARD OVER THE LAST 18 MONTHS, OR ENDURED THE LAST EIGHT YEARS, TO SUFFER THROUGH MORE FAILED LEADERSHIP.
NO WAY. NO HOW. NO MCCAIN.
BARACK OBAMA IS MY CANDIDATE. AND HE MUST BE OUR PRESIDENT.
FOR HER EFFORTS, DESPITE LOSING THE PRIMARY, HILLARY CLINTON WAS AWARDED THE POST OF SECRETARY OF STATE BY PRESIDENT ELECT OBAMA. HER SPIRIT OF HONEST COMPETITION, COUPLED WITH THE DIPLOMACY SHE SHOWED IN HER CONCESSION, MADE AN IMPRESSION ON THE PRESIDENT ELECT.

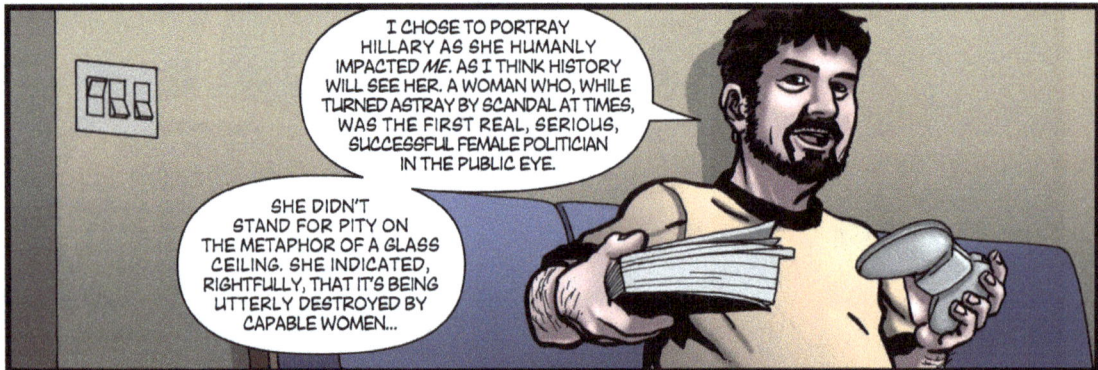

# AL FRANKEN

D. D. Max

AL FRANKEN HAS BEEN CALLED MANY THINGS

A COMEDIAN. A SELF-HELP GURU.

AN ACTOR.

A FATHER. A HUSBAND.

A RADIO HOST AND SMEAR MERCHANT.

A C-LIST CELEBRITY.

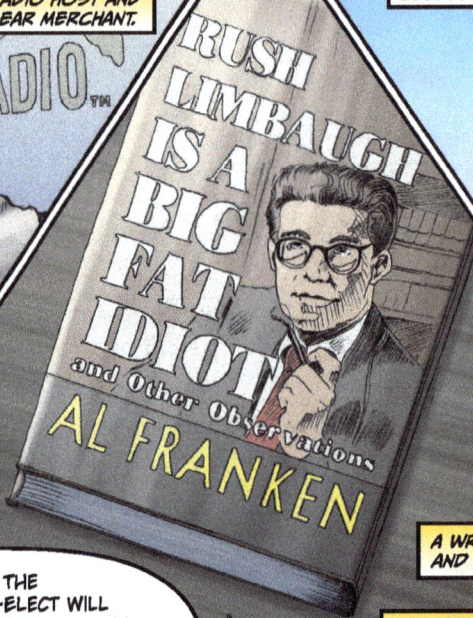

RUSH LIMBAUGH IS A BIG FAT IDIOT and Other Observations
AL FRANKEN

A WRITER AND SATIRIST.

IF THE SENATOR-ELECT WILL PRESENT HIMSELF AT THE DESK, THE CHAIR WILL ADMINISTER THE OATH OF OFFICE AS REQUIRED BY THE CONSTITUTION AND PRESCRIBED BY LAW. PLEASE RAISE YOUR RIGHT HAND.

BUT, AS OF JULY 7, 2009, THE ONE THING, REMARKABLY, THAT YOU CAN NOW CALL AL FRANKEN IS...

DO YOU SOLEMNLY SWEAR THAT YOU WILL SUPPORT AND DEFEND THE CONSTITUTION OF THE UNITED STATES AGAINST ALL ENEMIES, FOREIGN AND DOMESTIC, THAT YOU WILL BEAR TRUE FAITH AND ALLEGIANCE TO THE SAME, THAT YOU TAKE THIS OBLIGATION FREELY...

...WITHOUT ANY MENTAL RESERVATION OR PURPOSE OF EVASION AND THAT YOU WILL WELL AND FAITHFULLY DISCHARGE THE DUTIES OF THE OFFICE UPON WHICH YOU ARE ABOUT TO ENTER, SO HELP YOU GOD?

ALAN STUART FRANKEN WAS BORN ON MAY 21, 1951 IN NEW YORK CITY. HIS OLDER BROTHER OWEN WAS BORN IN 1946.

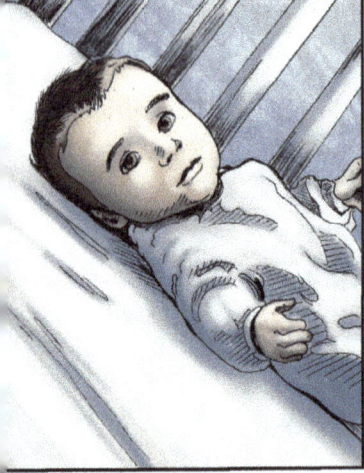

AL'S MIDDLE-CLASS PARENTS - JOE AND PHOEBE FRANKEN - MOVED TO MINNESOTA WHEN AL WAS FOUR.

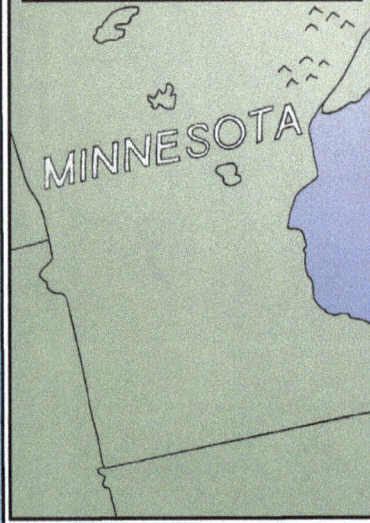

AL WAS AN EXTREMELY BRIGHT CHILD. HE WOULD EVENTUALLY SCORE A PERFECT 800 ON THE MATH SECTION OF HIS SATS AND BE ACCEPTED TO HARVARD.

MINNESOTA

AL'S DAD WORKED AS A PRINTING SALESMAN, THOUGH AL SAYS HE WASN'T A VERY GOOD ONE.

AL'S MOM GOT A REAL ESTATE LICENSE, WHERE SHE QUICKLY LEARNED ABOUT THE PRACTICE THAT WOULD LATER BECOME KNOWN AS REDLINING.

AL LEARNED THAT MEANT DEVELOPERS, BANKERS AND REAL ESTATE AGENTS HAD A SPOKEN OR UNSPOKEN AGREEMENT TO RESTRICT BLACKS OR JEWS FROM BUYING HOMES IN CERTAIN AREAS.

SO ON ONE SIDE OF A ROAD, YOU'D HAVE HOMES OWNED BY PEOPLE WITH NAMES LIKE ANDERSON, CARLSON, ANDERSON AGAIN AND RIGHT ACROSS THE STREET LIVING IN SIMILAR HOUSES WERE FAMILIES NAMED GOLDBERG, SHAPIRO AND GROSSMAN.

THIS WAS AN ESPECIALLY SHOCKING DISCOVERY, SINCE AL'S FAMILY HAD MOVED WHEN HE WAS SIX FROM THE SMALL TOWN OF ALBERT LEA TO THE MINNEAPOLIS SUBURB OF ST. LOUIS PARK.

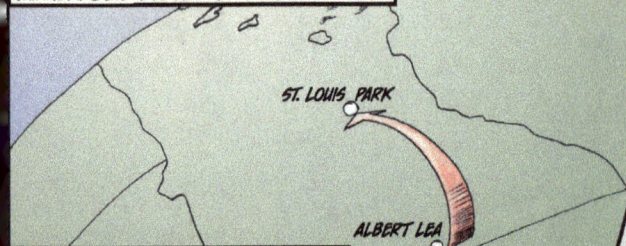

ST. LOUIS PARK

ALBERT LEA

IT WAS DUBBED "ST. JEWISH PARK" BECAUSE, BY MINNESOTA STANDARDS IT, HAD A LOT OF JEWS.

MINNEAPOLIS HAD A REPUTATION FOR ANTI-SEMITISM AT THE TIME, FUELED BY THE PRESENCE OF AN ORGANIZED CRIME SYNDICATE THAT HUBERT HUMPHREY CHASED OUT WHEN HE WAS MAYOR.

HIS MOM WOULD SHARE PAINFUL EXPERIENCES WITH HER SON - LIKE WHEN PEOPLE, UNAWARE OF HER CREED, SAID THEY WOULD NEVER BUY A HOME FROM A JEW.

THE 1960 PRESIDENTIAL ELECTION WAS A SOURCE OF FRICTION IN THE FRANKEN HOUSEHOLD.

WHEN THE FAMILY SAT IN FRONT OF THE TV WATCHING POLICE TURN DOGS AND FIRE HOSES ON BLACK DEMONSTRATORS, JOE AND PHOEBE WOULD COMPARE IT TO THE HOLOCAUST AND TELL THEIR SONS IT WAS THEIR DUTY AS JEWS TO SUPPORT CIVIL RIGHTS.

THIS HAD A PROFOUND EFFECT ON AL, AS HE SAW HIS FATHER LEAVE THE REPUBLICAN PARTY AND NEVER GO BACK.

PHOEBE, A DEMOCRAT, WAS FOR KENNEDY. SO WAS OWEN. JOE - A STEADFAST REPUBLICAN - WAS FOR NIXON, AS WAS AL.

HOWEVER, REPUBLICAN PRESIDENTIAL NOMINEE BARRY GOLDWATER'S OPPOSITION TO THE CIVIL RIGHTS ACT DURING THE 1964 CAMPAIGN CHANGED EVERYTHING FOR THE FRANKEN FAMILY.

A CARD-CARRYING MEMBER OF THE NAACP, JOE WAS DISGUSTED WITH GOLDWATER'S POSITION.

SAW A MAN WHO VOTED FOR EVERY REPUBLICAN FROM HERBERT HOOVER TO RICHARD NIXON TURN AROUND AND VOTE FOR EVERY DEMOCRAT FROM LYNDON JOHNSON TO BILL CLINTON, UNTIL HIS DEATH IN 1993.

AL GRADUATED FROM HIGH SCHOOL IN 1969, HAVING ATTENDED THE BLAKE SCHOOL IN MINNEAPOLIS.

IN 1971, ONE OF AL'S MAIN MISSIONS WAS TO HELP OWEN AVOID THE DRAFT FOR VIETNAM BY MAKING SURE HE WAS UNDERWEIGHT. AL HAD ALREADY RECEIVED A DEFERMENT BECAUSE HE WAS ATTENDING HARVARD.

HAVING WRESTLED IN HIGH SCHOOL, AL KNEW HOW TO LOSE WEIGHT – AND HAD A SPECIAL MOTIVATIONAL TECHNIQUE HE USED WHENEVER HE THOUGHT OWEN WAS SLACKING.

GET UP! CHARLIE'S COMING! CHARLIE'S COMING TO GET YA!

OWEN FRANKEN WEIGHED 109 POUNDS AT HIS PHYSICAL AND NEVER HAD TO FACE THE VIET CONG.

AL MET FRANNI BRYSTON DURING HIS FIRST WEEK AT HARVARD AT A MIXER AT SIMMONS COLLEGE. SHE WAS 17 AND HE WAS 18.

FRANNI AND AL WERE MARRIED ON OCTOBER 2, 1975.

1975 WAS A VERY MOMENTOUS YEAR FOR AL, WHO WAS RECRUITED BY LORNE MICHAELS ALONG WITH PROFESSIONAL PARTNER TOM DAVIS TO WRITE FOR A NEW SHOW CALLED "SATURDAY NIGHT LIVE".

"SNL" GAVE FRANKEN THE OPPORTUNITY TO WRITE FOR AND PERFORM WITH BREAKOUT STARS LIKE BILL MURRAY, JOHN BELUSHI, GILDA RADNER AND DAN AYKROYD.

DURING A ONE WEEK BREAK FROM THE SHOW THAT OCTOBER, OWEN – NOW A PROFESSIONAL PHOTOGRAPHER – INVITED AL ON THE PRESS BUS WITH HIM IN NEW HAMPSHIRE TO FOLLOW RONALD REAGAN.

REAGAN, WHO WAS CHALLENGING PRESIDENT FORD FOR THE GOP NOMINATION, INTRIGUED FRANKEN BECAUSE HE HAD OPPOSED THE CIVIL RIGHTS ACT BY USING THE RATIONALE THAT YOU CAN'T LEGISLATE MORALITY.

THE BROTHERS' FIRST STOP WAS CAMBRIDGE, MASSACHUSETTS. MO UDALL WAS SPEAKING AT MIT, OWEN'S ALMA MATER.

A BORING SPEAKER AND A LATE CANDIDATE HAD THE CROWD RESTLESS.

THE CROWD WENT NUTS. IT WAS LIKELY THE BEST RECEPTION UDALL WOULD RECEIVE DURING THE ENTIRE CAMPAIGN.

OWEN, HOWEVER, WAS LESS THAN PLEASED.

DON'T EVER DO THAT AGAIN.

LADIES AND GENTLEMEN! THE NEXT PRESIDENT OF THE UNITED STATES! MO UDALL!

AL DECIDED TO STEP TO THE PODIUM AND ENTERTAIN THE CROWD. WHEN UDALL FINALLY ARRIVED, HE TOOK IT UPON HIMSELF TO INTRODUCE HIM.

A FEW DAYS LATER, AL AND OWEN FOLLOWED REAGAN AROUND SEVERAL EVENTS IN NEW HAMPSHIRE, WHERE MANDATORY MOTORCYCLE HELMETS AND DECRIMINALIZING MARIJUANA HAD BECOME BIG ISSUES.

BY THE LAST EVENT AT THE DARTMOUTH HOCKEY ARENA, AL COULD NO LONGER STAY NEUTRAL AND CLIMBED OVER THE ROPE SEPARATING THE PRESS AND PUBLIC TO GET IN LINE AND ASK A QUESTION.

I'VE BEEN FOLLOWING YOU ON THE PRESS BUS ALL DAY AND THIS MORNING IN DERBY FALLS YOU SAID YOU WERE AGAINST MANDATORY MOTORCYCLE HELMETS BECAUSE IT'S A LIMIT TO PERSONAL FREEDOM.

BOOOOO!

AND THEN LATER THIS AFTERNOON IN CORNISH FLAT YOU SAID YOU WERE AGAINST DECRIMINALIZING MARIJUANA BECAUSE IT CAUSES BRAIN DAMAGE.

BOOOOO!

WHAT'S YOUR QUESTION?

WELL, CAN'T NOT WEARING A MOTORCYCLE HELMET CAUSE BRAIN DAMAGE A LOT QUICKER THAN MARIJUANA BY, FOR EXAMPLE...

...THE HEAD SPLITTING OPEN SO THAT ACTUAL MATERIAL FROM THE ROAD ENTERS THE BRAIN?

BOOOOO!

WELL, IF I WAS ON AN AIRPLANE AND THE PILOT WAS DRUNK I'D BE ABLE TO TELL. BUT IF HE WAS HIGH ON MARIJUANA, I WOULDN'T. BE ABLE TO TELL.

APPLAUSE

LYN NOFZIGER, WHO RAN THE PRESS BUS, WAS NOT PLEASED.

EITHER YOU'RE A MEMBER OF THE PRESS OR YOU'RE A MEMBER OF THE PUBLIC!

AL WAS KICKED OFF THE BUS FOR CROSSING THE LINE.

THOUGH AL BEAT THE BUS BACK TO THE HOTEL, WHEN OWEN GOT OFF HE ACTED LIKE HE DIDN'T KNOW AL – AND DECIDED TO PUT AN END TO THEIR FRATERNAL CAMPAIGN JUNKETS.

AL CALLED SILVERMAN "A TOTAL UNEQUIVOCAL FAILURE" IN THE SKETCH, WHILE HOLDING UP A GRAPH SHOWING THE NETWORK'S PRIME-TIME RATINGS PLUMMETING.

AL'S PROPENSITY FOR GOING OVER THE LINE HAD A DRAMATIC EFFECT ON "SNL" IN 1980.

IN A SKETCH TITLED "A LIMO FOR A LAMO", AL LAUNCHED A BLISTERING ATTACK ON NBC PRESIDENT FRED SILVERMAN.

SILVERMAN WAS NOT AMUSED AND TOOK OUT HIS ANGER ON MICHAELS.

THIS LED TO MICHAELS' DEPARTURE FROM "SNL" AT SEASON'S END, ALONG WITH FRANKEN AND THE REST OF THE CAST.

A BUNDLE OF JOY WOULD ENTER AL'S LIFE IN 1981 WHEN HE AND FRANNI'S FIRST CHILD, DAUGHTER THOMASIN, WAS BORN.

HOWEVER, THE EARLY 1980S CONTINUED TO BE A TUMULTUOUS TIME IN AL'S LIFE.

BESIDES NO LONGER HAVING A STEADY "SNL" PAYCHECK TO COUNT ON, HE HAD TO DEAL WITH FRANNI'S GROWING ALCOHOLISM.

ANDY GARCIA

MEG RYA

AL EVENTUALLY WENT TO AL-ANON MEETINGS IN 1987 TO HELP HIM DEAL WITH FRANNI'S ALCOHOLISM.

SUBSTANCE ABUSE PROBLEMS HAD ALREADY COST HIM HIS LONGTIME PROFESSIONAL PARTNERSHIP WITH DAVIS. BUT HE WAS DETERMINED TO STAND BY HIS WIFE.

SHE EVENTUALLY RECOVERED AND AL USED THEIR MUTUAL STRUGGLE AND TRIUMPH AS THE BASIS FOR THE 1994 FILM "WHEN A MAN LOVES A WOMAN", STARRING ANDY GARCIA AND MEG RYAN, WHICH HE CO-PRODUCED AND CO-WROTE.

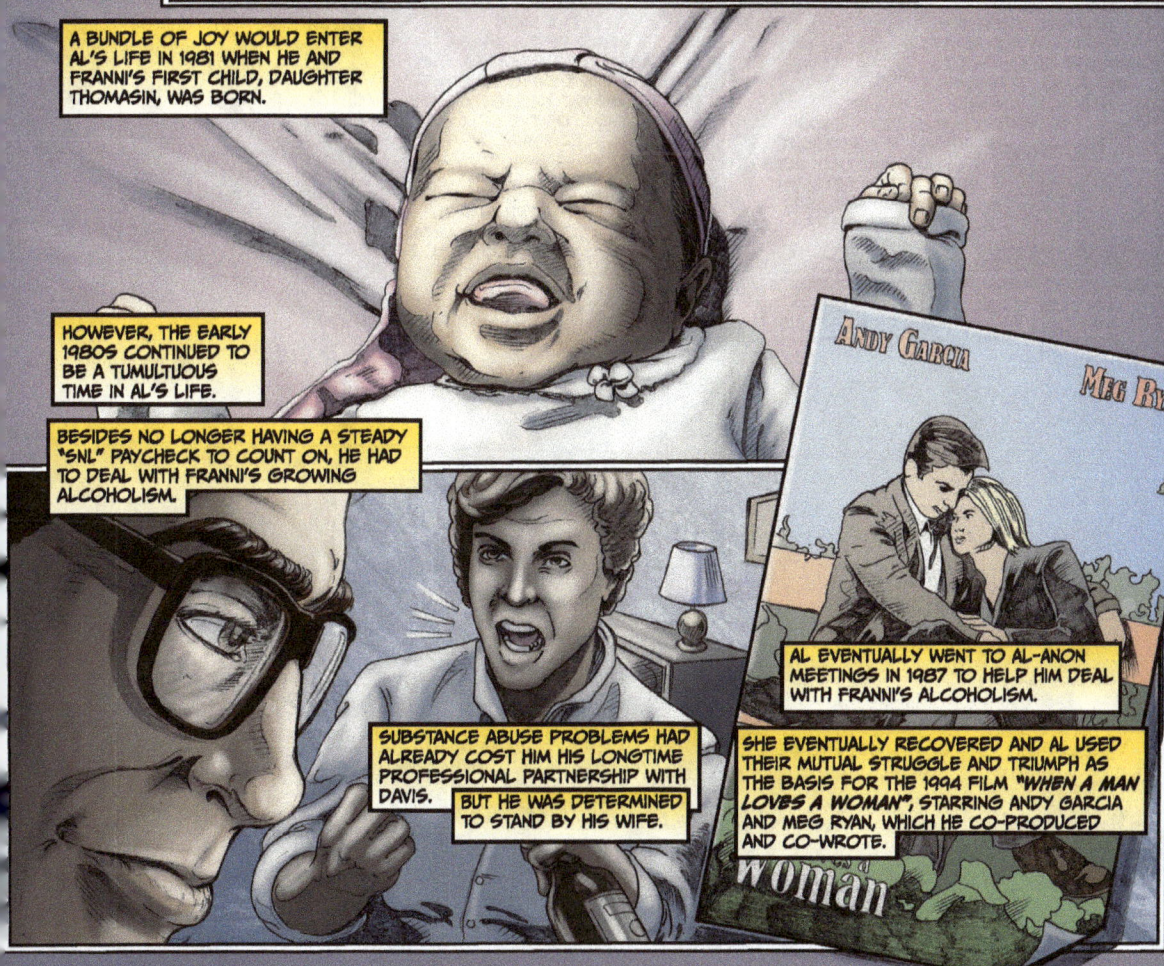

woman

**I'M GOOD ENOUGH, I'M SMART ENOUGH AND DOGGONE IT, PEOPLE LIKE ME!**

AL RETURNED TO *"SATURDAY NIGHT LIVE"* IN 1985 AND WOULD REMAIN WITH THE SHOW FOR ANOTHER DECADE. COUNTING BOTH HIS STINTS, AL WON FIVE EMMYS WHILE WITH *"SNL".*

DURING THIS STINT WITH THE SHOW, AL BECAME BEST KNOWN FOR HIS CHARACTER STUART SMALLEY.

AL WAS INSPIRED TO CREATE SMALLEY, A SELF-HELP GURU AND MEMBER OF SEVERAL 12-STEP PROGRAMS, BY ATTENDING AL-ANON.

1986 WAS ALSO THE YEAR AL STARTED EMCEEING FUNDRAISERS FOR DEMOCRAT MARK GREEN, WHO WAS SEEKING THE SENATE SEAT HELD BY REPUBLICAN AL D'AMATO.

AL QUICKLY BECAME KNOWN FOR HAVING AN IRREVERENT STYLE.

**I'D GO TO AL-ANON, WHICH IS FOR FRIENDS AND FAMILY MEMBERS OF ALCOHOLICS, AND GOING TO AL-ANON MEETINGS INSPIRED STUART.**

**STUART WAS ABOUT - YOU KNOW - IT WAS ABOUT RECOVERY AND THAT GOES INTO A LOT OF DIFFERENT AREAS OF LIFE AND I'VE BEEN VERY GRATIFIED.**

**I'VE BEEN ASKED BY THE GREEN CAMPAIGN TO ANNOUNCE THAT THE VIEWS I EXPRESS TONIGHT ARE MINE AND NOT NECESSARILY THOSE OF THE GREEN CAMPAIGN.**

**OKAY, NOW THAT THAT'S OUT OF THE WAY - ISN'T CARDINAL O'CONNOR AN ASSHOLE?**

HA HA HA

IN 1986, AL SAW HIS FAMILY EXPAND BY ONE, AS JOE FRANKEN WAS BORN.

GREEN KEPT TELLING AL NOT TO DO IT, AL WOULD ANYWAY.

GREEN WOULD END UP LOSING THE ELECTION, BUT AL'S POLITICAL STAR WAS RISING.

AL WOULD GO ON TO PROVIDE COMMENTARY FOR CNN AT THE 1988 DEMOCRATIC NATIONAL CONVENTION.

ON NOVEMBER 8, 1988 AL EMCEED THE MICHAEL DUKAKIS VICTORY CELEBRATION.

LADIES AND GENTLEMEN, I'VE PREPARED TWO KINDS OF MATERIAL.

ONE IN CASE WE WIN BY A SQUEAKER –

AND THE OTHER, IN CASE... WE WIN BY A LANDSLIDE!

NO ONE LAUGHED AT WHAT WAS NOW GALLOWS HUMOR. IN WHAT WAS NOW BECOMING A QUADRENNIAL RITUAL, DEMOCRAT MICHAEL DUKAKIS WAS ON HIS WAY TO BEING SOUNDLY BEATEN BY REPUBLICAN GEORGE H.W. BUSH IN THE RACE FOR THE WHITE HOUSE.

Dukakis Bentsen

POLLS HADN'T CLOSED ANYWHERE, BUT THESE DEMOCRATS WHO HAD PUT THEIR LIVES ON HOLD TO ELECT THEIR CANDIDATE FOR PRESIDENT ALL KNEW.

AND AL HAD TO ENTERTAIN AN INCREASINGLY DEPRESSED GROUP OF PEOPLE FOR FOUR HOURS.

Ohio  Pennsylvania

PENNSYLVANIA GOES FOR BUSH! OHIO GOES FOR BUSH!

HEY, WE WON RHODE ISLAND! THAT'S GOOD. AS RHODE ISLAND GOES, SO GOES THE NATION. RIGHT? HUH, EVERYBODY?

BUSH TAKES OHIO   CNN

THE COMIC HIGH POINT OF THE EVENING WAS AN APPEARANCE BY AL'S "SNL" COLLEAGUE JON LOVITZ.

AMONG THE ALL-TIME GREAT "SNL" MOMENTS WAS THE BUSH-DUKAKIS DEBATE SKETCH, IN WHICH DANA CARVEY PLAYED A PERIPATETIC GEORGE BUSH TO JON'S EMOTIONALLY INERT MICHAEL DUKAKIS.

LADIES AND GENTLEMEN, IT IS MY DISTINCT HONOR TO INTRODUCE THE GOVERNOR OF MASSACHUSETTS, THE LEADER OF OUR PARTY, MICHAEL S. DUKAKIS!

IF HE DID THAT TO BARBARA, THINK WHAT HE'LL DO TO THE COUNTRY!

BUT LOVITZ, UNLIKE FRANKEN IS NOT A POLITICAL SATIRIST AND MOST OF HIS JOKES FELL FLAT.

THOUGH DISAPPOINTED IN THE RESULT, AL CONSOLED HIMSELF WITH THE BELIEF THAT THE PEOPLE HAD SPOKEN.

HOWEVER, HE NOTICED JON LOOKED VERY UPSET.

I KNOW. IT'S A BIG DISAPPOINTMENT.

YEAH. NOW FUCKING DANA GETS TO PLAY THE FUCKING PRESIDENT FOR THE NEXT FOUR YEARS.

THEN, HE WAS INVITED TO A VERY EXCLUSIVE EVENT CALLED RENAISSANCE WEEKEND, WHERE HE PLAYED TOUCH FOOTBALL WITH THE WINNER OF THAT ELECTION, PRESIDENT BILL CLINTON.

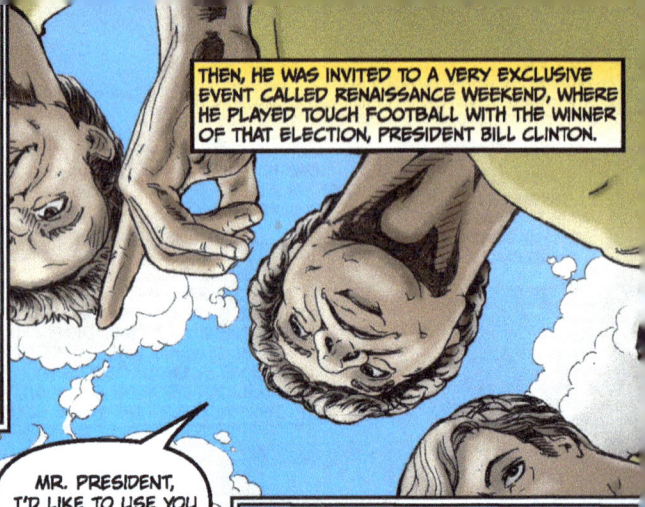

MR. PRESIDENT, I'D LIKE TO USE YOU AS A DECOY.

UH, OKAY.

AL'S PLAY WORKED, IMPRESSING NOT ONLY THE PRESIDENT BUT FRANNI AS WELL.

NEXT, IN APRIL 1994, AL WAS INVITED TO SPEAK AT THE WHITE HOUSE CORRESPONDENTS DINNER.

THIS MEANT HE GOT TO HAVE COCKTAILS WITH THE GORES AND THE CLINTONS, A PRIVILEGE THAT WOULD NORMALLY COST A FORTUNE.

TIPPER, I GOT THIS JOKE ABOUT YOUR HUSBAND AND MY INSTINCT IS THAT IT MIGHT BE OVER THE LINE. I WAS WONDERING IF I COULD RUN IT BY YOU.

OKAY. LET'S HEAR IT.

OKAY. HERE'S THE JOKE. VICE-PRESIDENT GORE CONTINUED TO SHOW HIS COMMITMENT TO THE ENVIRONMENT BY ANNOUNCING TODAY THAT HE'S GOING TO CHANGE THE POLICY ON THE STICK UP HIS BUTT.

INSTEAD OF REPLACING THE STICK EVERY DAY WITH A NEW STICK, THE VICE-PRESIDENT WILL KEEP THE SAME STICK UP HIS BUTT FOR THE REST OF THE ADMINISTRATION. EVIDENTLY, THIS WILL SAVE AN ENTIRE RAIN FOREST.

I'D GO WITH YOUR INSTINCT.

AL DID AND HIS MONOLOGUE GOT GREAT REVIEWS.

THE NEXT YEAR, AT THE 1995 WHITE HOUSE CORRESPONDENTS DINNER, CONAN O'BRIEN ASKED AL FOR ADVICE FOR HIS MONOLOGUE.

I WANT TO JOKE THAT THE ENTERTAINMENT TONIGHT WAS GOING TO BE ME, OR SENATOR D'AMATO DOING IMPRESSIONS.

WHY DON'T YOU CHANGE IT TO, 'THE CHOICE WAS EITHER ME OR SENATOR D'AMATO DOING AN IMPRESSION OF A JAPANESE GUY HAVING A HEART ATTACK'?

AL FELT NEW YORK SENATOR AL D'AMATO WOULD MAKE A PRIME TARGET. A FEW WEEKS EARLIER HE HAD DONE AN OVER-THE-TOP JAPANESE STEREOTYPE IMPRESSION OF JUDGE LANCE ITO. THE RESULTANT CONTROVERSY CAUSED STRESS THAT HAD LIKELY CONTRIBUTED TO D'AMATO BEING RUSHED TO THE HOSPITAL WITH HEART PALPITATIONS.

FOR DINNER, AL GOT TO SIT NEXT TO THE BEAUTIFUL, RICH, POWERFUL ARIANNA HUFFINGTON. HE LEARNED DURING THEIR CONVERSATION THAT SHE WAS RAISING MONEY FOR HOUSE SPEAKER NEWT GINGRICH.

HUFFINGTON PROCEEDED TO INTRODUCE AL TO THE SPEAKER, WHO WAS ACTUALLY HAPPY WITH A SKIT IN WHICH CHRIS FARLEY PORTRAYED HIM.

I HAD NOTHING TO DO WITH THAT, BUT CHRIS HAD A REALLY GOOD TIME AND COULDN'T TALK ABOUT ANYTHING ELSE FOR THE WHOLE WEEK.

NOW, CAN I ASK YOU SOMETHING? I BELIEVE IN THE MARKET SYSTEM. BUT I THINK THAT, AT THE END OF THE DAY, WHAT YOU'RE DOING WILL LEAD TO A SITUATION WHERE THE STATES ARE FORCED TO COMPETE WITH EACH OTHER TO DRIVE OUT THEIR POOR BY LOWERING BENEFITS.

WHAT'S WRONG WITH THAT?

SO, NATURALLY, AL SPENT MUCH OF DINNER RAGGING ON HIM.

WHAT KIND OF SLEAZEBAG DOESN'T SUPPORT HIS KIDS.

SHE'S VERY ANTI-SEMITIC AND VERY ANTI-RACIST.

CAN I QUOTE YOU ON THAT?

AL AND GINGRICH'S CONVERSATION SOON TURNED TO CHRISTINA JEFFREY, THE WOMAN GINGRICH HAD CHOSEN AS HOUSE HISTORIAN, THEN DROPPED LIKE A HOT POTATO WHEN IT WAS DISCLOSED THAT SHE HAD ONCE OBJECTED TO A COURSE ON THE HOLOCAUST BECAUSE IT FAILED TO PRESENT THE NAZI AND KU KLUX KLAN POINTS OF VIEW.

YET HE STILL DEFENDED HER.

DO YOU REALIZE WHAT YOU JUST SAID?

I MEANT ANTI-ANTI-SEMITIC.

YEAH, I GET THEM MIXED UP ALL THE TIME.

AFTER DINNER, AL HEADED OVER TO A HIP PARTY THROWN BY 'VANITY FAIR' MAGAZINE AND SAW SEN. D'AMATO.

WHICH MEANT HIS FUN HAD JUST BEGUN.

HE'S FROM "SATURDAY NIGHT LIVE"!

OKAY. MAYBE IT WASN'T FAIR TO YOUR SISTER, BUT IT WAS FAIR TO YOU.

I DON'T KNOW. MY SISTAH HAVING SEX WITH A DONKEY? I DON'T REALLY SEE WHAT WAS SO WRONG WITH WHAT I DID IN THE FIRST PLACE.

WHAT WAS THAT THING ABOUT MY SISTAH HAVING SEX WITH A DONKEY?

WELL, YOU KNOW, I THOUGHT IT WAS FAIR. IT WAS ITO RESPONDING TO SOMETHING YOU'VE ADMITTED WAS A MISTAKE.

WHILE WE'RE ON THE SUBJECT, I WROTE A JOKE ABOUT YOU FOR CONAN BUT HE DIDN'T USE IT.

NO. HE USED IT. I THOUGHT IT WAS FUNNY.

THEN, DEEP DOWN, YOU PROBABLY THOUGHT IT WAS FAIR.

WELL, I ADMIT, I DID THINK IT WAS FUNNY.

BUT MY SISTAH?

A COUPLE WEEKS EARLIER, AN "SNL" CAST MEMBER HAD DONE A PIECE IN WHICH JUDGE ITO RESPONDS TO D'AMATO'S IMPRESSION WITH AN IMPRESSION OF D'AMATO'S SISTER HAVING SEX WITH DONKEY.

ACTUALLY, NBC SENSORS HAD MADE AL AND THE OTHER "SNL" WRITERS CHANGE THE SKIT FROM HIS MOTHER HAVING SEX WITH A DONKEY TO HIS SISTER, SINCE THEY THOUGHT THAT WOULD BE IN SLIGHTLY BETTER TASTE.

YEAH, WELL, I HAD A VARIATION. IT WENT, 'THE ENTERTAINMENT TONIGHT WAS EITHER GOING TO BE ME OR SENATOR D'AMATO DOING HIS IMPRESSION OF A JAPANESE GUY HAVING A HEART ATTACK.

D'AMATO AND HIS FIANCE WERE STUNNED SPEECHLESS.

AL WAS QUICKLY BECOMING MAD AS HELL AND NOT WILLING TO TAKE IT ANYMORE.

ONE SIGN OF THIS IS WHEN HE ENDED HIS SECOND STINT ON "SNL" IN 1995 AFTER BEING REJECTED AS "WEEKEND UPDATE" ANCHOR IN FAVOR OF NORM MACDONALD.

AL HAD BEEN LOOKING TO FOCUS HIS ENERGIES MORE IN THE POLITICAL WORLD ANYWAY!

HIS ONLY QUESTION WAS, 'WHO OR WHAT SHOULD I FOCUS ON?'

IT'S ME, RUSH LIMBAUGH, WITH TALENT ON LOAN FROM GOD!

FEMINISM WAS ESTABLISHED SO THAT UNATTRACTIVE, UGLY WOMEN COULD HAVE EASY ACCESS TO THE MAINSTREAM OF SOCIETY.

LIBERALS LOVE MISERY. IT MAKES THEM FEEL NECESSARY.

LIBERALS DON'T WANT THE HOMELESS TO HOLD A JOB THAT HAS ANY REAL PROMISE.

YOU ARE MORALLY SUPERIOR TO THOSE LIBERAL COMPASSION FASCISTS. YOU HAVE A REAL JOB. THEY JUST BEG FOR A LIVING.

THE POOR IN THIS COUNTRY ARE THE BIGGEST PIGLETS AT THE MOTHER PIG AND HER NIPPLES. THE POOR FEED OFF THE LARGESSE OF THIS GOVERNMENT AND GIVE NOTHING BACK.

HOW DOES THIS GUY GET AWAY WITH THIS STUFF!?!

ACTUALLY, THE ULTRA-CONSERVATIVE, SUPER-POPULAR TALK RADIO ICON FIRST CAUGHT AL'S ATTENTION WHEN HE WAS WATCHING HIS TV SHOW. RUSH MADE A MEMORABLE JOKE.

DID YOU KNOW THE CLINTONS NOT ONLY HAVE A WHITE HOUSE CAT-

ON A NATIONALLY SYNDICATED PROGRAM, RUSH LIMBAUGH HAD JUST INSULTED A 13-YEAR-OLD GIRL REGARDING HER LOOKS.

- BUT THEY ALSO HAVE A WHITE HOUSE DOG.

A YEAR LATER HE WOULD BE CALLED THE "MAJORITY MAKER" AS HIS 20 MILLION LISTENERS WERE CREDITED WITH PLAYING A LARGE ROLE IN THE REPUBLICANS TAKING CONTROL OF CONGRESS FOR THE FIRST TIME IN 40 YEARS.

AL FELT IT WAS TIME FOR SOMEONE TO COME UP WITH A FUNNY, IN-YOUR-FACE MANIFESTO.

IN 1996, "RUSH LIMBAUGH IS A BIG FAT IDIOT AND OTHER OBSERVATIONS" HIT BOOKSTORES. IT'S IMPACT WAS HUGE.

RUSH LIMBAUGH IS A BIG FAT IDIOT

AL HAD NOT ONLY STOOD UP TO THE BIGGEST BULLY ON THE CONSERVATIVE BLOCK WITH THE TOME, BUT THROUGH PAINSTAKING RESEARCH WAS TAKING THE FIGHT TO HIM AND HITTING HARD.

FRANKEN

HE SOON FOUND HIMSELF CONFRONTED BY ANOTHER ANGRY IRISHMAN AFTERWARD.

FOX NEWS STAR SEAN HANNITY DID NOT LIKE THE TITLE OF AL'S BOOK.

I DON'T BELIEVE IN MAKING AD HOMINEM ATTACKS.

OH. THAT'S WHY I TITLED IT "RUSH LIMBAUGH IS A BIG FAT IDIOT". IT'S AN IRONIC COMMENT ON THE FACT THAT RUSH MAKES AD HOMINEM ATTACKS ALL THE TIME. YOU SEE?

I'VE NEVER HEARD HIM MAKE AN AD HOMINEM ATTACK.

REALLY? HOW ABOUT WHEN HE CALLED CHELSEA CLINTON "THE WHITE HOUSE DOG"? WOULD THAT QUALIFY?

THAT WAS A MISTAKE. A TECHNICIAN ACCIDENTALLY PUT UP THE WRONG PICTURE.

REALLY? OKAY, THEN TELL ME, WHAT WAS THE JOKE? "THE CLINTONS NOT ONLY HAVE A WHITE HOUSE CAT - PICTURE OF SOCKS - "THEY HAVE A WHITE HOUSE DOG". WHAT'S THE JOKE? WHAT PICTURE WAS SUPPOSED TO COME UP?

YOU KNOW, HE'S GOT A POINT, SEAN. THERE'S NO JOKE WITHOUT THE PICTURE OF CHELSEA.

IT WAS A MISTAKE! A TECHNICIAN PUT UP THE WRONG PICTURE! THAT'S WHAT RUSH SAID! AND I BELIEVE RUSH!

OKAY! LET ME ASK YOU THIS! IT WAS A TAPED SHOW!

TAPED HOURS BEFORE IT AIRED! IF IT WAS A TECHNICAL MISTAKE, WHY DIDN'T THEY FIX IT WITH THE CORRECT PICTURE, WHATEVER THAT POSSIBLY COULD HAVE BEEN?

YOU'RE BEING INTELLECTUALLY DISHONEST!

INTELLECTUAL DISHONESTY? HOW ABOUT THE DEMOCRATS SAYING GINGRICH WANTS TO CUT MEDICARE SPENDING?

YOU'RE CHANGING THE SUBJECT, SEAN.

WHEN ACTUALLY IT'S A SEVEN PERCENT INCREASE IN SPENDING! INCREASE!

RIGHT. LOOK, COULD YOU JUST ADMIT THAT RUSH DELIBERATELY INSULTED A 13-YEAR-

I MEAN, TALK ABOUT INTELLECTUAL DISHONESTY!

COLMES WOULD SEPARATE THE TWO MEN.

HANNITY WOULD REPORT AL HAD BEEN "ESCORTED OUT BY FOX SECURITY".

AL WOULD LATER SAY HE NEVER IN HIS LIFE HATED ANYONE THE WAY HE HATED SEAN HANNITY AT THAT MOMENT.

BUT IT LAID THE GROUNDWORK FOR TWO OF THE THREE BRICKS THAT WOULD SERVE AS THE FOUNDATION FOR SUCCESSFUL WRITING AND POLITICAL CAREERS: THE ABILITY AND WILLINGNESS TO CONFRONT CONSERVATIVE PUNDITS AND POLITICIANS (ESPECIALLY IRISH ONES) AND A RIVALRY WITH FOX NEWS.

FOX NEWS Channel

LITTLE DID AL KNOW AT THE TIME, BUT IT WOULD ALL START WITH SEEMINGLY THE LEAST LIKELY CANDIDATE OF ALL - BARBARA BUSH.

PERHAPS THE MOST POPULAR FIRST LADY IN RECENT TIMES, BARBARA ALWAYS SEEMED TO HAVE THE AURA OF BEING A MATRONLY GRANDMOTHER, THE BENEVOLENT BUSH FAMILY MATRIARCH WHO STAYED ABOVE THE FRAY.

AL WAS ABOUT TO FIND OUT THE REALITY WAS QUITE DIFFERENT.

THE OTHER BRICK IN THE FOUNDATION WOULD BE THE BUSH FAMILY.

SPECIFICALLY, HIS DISAGREEMENTS WITH AND INCREASING CONTEMPT FOR THE BUSH FAMILY.

EXCUSE ME, MRS. BUSH. MY NAME IS AL FRANKEN AND I'M A FRIEND OF DANA CARVEY'S.

OH. WELL, DANA'S A GOOD MAN.

DANA, OF COURSE, HAD DONE A HILARIOUS, IF AT TIMES UNFLATTERING IMPRESSION OF BARBARA'S HUSBAND, GEORGE H.W. BUSH ON "SNL" THE BUSHES HAD GRACEFULLY INVITED DANA TO THE WHITE HOUSE AFTER THE 1992 ELECTION AND BY ALL REPORTS THEY HAD GOTTEN ALONG.

I'LL BET DANA MISSES MY HUSBAND.

YES. BUT I'M SURE HE'S WORKING ON YOUR SON.

WHEN HE LAUGHS SOMETIMES, HIS SHOULDERS GO UP AND DOWN LIKE THIS.

AL HAD NOTICED A SMALL QUIRK WITH "DUBYA" THAT WILL FERRELL WOULD EVENTUALLY MAKE FAMOUS.

HEH.HEH. HEH.

I'VE NEVER SEEN HIM DO THAT.

WELL, I'M SURE DANA WILL DO IT BETTER. AND OF COURSE, IT'S GOING TO BE A *VERY* VALUABLE IMPRESSION.

YOU KNOW. UNTIL NOVEMBER.

SHORTLY AFTER HIS EXPERIENCE WITH BARBARA BUSH, AL ATTENDED THE BAT MITZVAH OF A FRIEND'S DAUGHTER.

SHE'S THE ENFORCER!

OMIGOD, SHE'S THE WORST BITCH ON EARTH!

SHE CAN BE VERY CHARMING, BUT BARBARA BUSH IS THE QUEEN BITCH!

SHE'S MEAN, BUT SHE KEEPS EVERYONE IN LINE!

OH, NO! SHE'S A HORRIBLE BITCH!

BARBARA'S THE TOUGH ONE!

THE FRIEND WAS AN EXTREMELY WELL-REGARDED POLITICAL JOURNALIST WHO HAD WRITTEN ABOUT THE BUSHES FOR YEARS, OFTEN IN GLOWING TERMS.

MANY OF THE GUESTS WOULD BE OTHER WASHINGTON INSIDERS, DEMOCRATS AND REPUBLICANS ALIKE. THEY WOULD KNOW IF MRS. BUSH HAD BEEN KIDDING

AL GOT A UNANIMOUS RESPONSE. THEY THOUGHT IT WAS FUNNY HE THOUGHT SHE HAD BEEN KIDDING.

BUT ANOTHER, MORE INTERESTING INSIGHT CAME FROM EVERYONE WHO KNEW THE BUSHES.

THEY SAID "DUBYA" WAS DEFINITELY HER SON.

THAT IS, DESPITE APPEARING LIKABLE, HE WAS MEAN.

AL HAD FIRST MET GEORGE W. BUSH THE YEAR BEFORE WHILE COVERING THE IOWA STRAW POLL FOR "GEORGE" MAGAZINE.

IOWA

HE HAD FOUND HIM CHARMING.

THIS WAS A PERIOD WHERE RUMORS OF BUSH'S COCAINE USE HAD FIRST COME OUT AND WHICH HE HAD REFUSED TO ANSWER.

GOVERNOR, I PERSONALLY DON'T CARE ABOUT WHETHER OR NOT YOU DID COCAINE YEARS AGO WHEN YOU WERE A YOUNG MAN.

BUT SINCE WE'RE IN IOWA, I FEEL I HAVE TO ASK YOU IF YOU'VE EVER MANUFACTURED ANY CRYSTAL METH.

HEH. HEH. HEH.

AL FELT IT WAS NOT ONLY CHARMING THAT BUSH HAD LAUGHED AT HIS QUESTION, BUT IMPORTANT.

BECAUSE HE DIDN'T BELIEVE FOR A MOMENT THAT BUSH HAD EVER COOKED A TUB OF METHAMPHETAMINES.

IF HE HAD ANSWERED THE QUESTION, AL COULD HAVE TRAPPED HIM SINCE HE HAD REFUSED TO ANSWER QUESTIONS ABOUT THE COCAINE RUMORS. BY SIMPLY LAUGHING, BUSH HAD OUTSMARTED HIM.

AFTER BUSH WON THE ELECTION AND AL FOUND HIS POLICIES INCREASINGLY REPUGNANT, HE REALIZED BUSH'S CHARM HAD THE EFFECT OF PEOPLE BLAMING EVERYONE BUT HIM.

HE FELT PEOPLE WERE ALL TOO READY TO DEMONIZE KARL ROVE, DICK CHENEY, DONALD RUMSFELD OR JOHN ASHCROFT OR OTHERS WHEN THE ADMINISTRATION DID SOMETHING THEY FELT WAS DESPICABLE.

HOWEVER, LIKE HIS MOTHER BARBARA, AL FELT BUSH WAS MEAN UNDERNEATH.

HE FELT PEOPLE SHOULDN'T KID THEMSELVES. "IT ALL CAME FROM BUSH", HE CONCLUDED. "BECAUSE HE'S BARBARA BUSH'S SON AND HE'S MEAN."

AND AL WOULD INCREASINGLY FEEL HE WAS THROUGH WITH HIM.

LIKE MOST AMERICANS, AL UNITED BEHIND PRESIDENT BUSH IN THE AFTERMATH OF THE TERRORIST ATTACKS ON 9/11.

I THINK ALL AMERICANS REMEMBER HOW WE FELT ON 9/12. WE WERE ALL AMERICANS. WE WERE ALL UNITED.

WE REALLY WERE AND NOT ONLY THAT BUT THE WORLD, VIRTUALLY THE ENTIRE WORLD, WAS BEHIND US AND BUSH WAS HANDED THIS OPPORTUNITY, THIS GOLDEN OPPORTUNITY ON A SILVER PLATTER TO LEAD.

IF WE HAD A REAL LEADER THEN SOMEONE WOULD HAVE UNITED AMERICA AND THE WORLD BEHIND US, COULD HAVE IN A SPIRIT OF SACRIFICE, MUTUAL PURPOSE AND MUTUAL UNDERSTANDING REALLY HAVE LED THE WORLD, AND HE BLEW IT BY HIJACKING 9/11 FOR HIS OWN PETTY POLITICAL PURPOSES. AND I'LL NEVER FORGIVE HIM OR THAT.

IN 2002, AL ALSO GAVE THE BUSH ADMINISTRATION THE BENEFIT OF THE DOUBT REGARDING IT'S JUSTIFICATION FOR THE IMPENDING IRAQ WAR.

IRAQ

AL FELT SADDAM WAS EVIL, IS GLAD WE GOT RID OF HIM AND FEELS TODAY THE IRAQI PEOPLE ARE BETTER OFF WITHOUT HIM.

AL AND HIS BROTHER OWEN EVEN LIT A MENORAH TO CELEBRATE HANUKAH IN AN "OBSCENELY LARGE" FOYER IN SADDAM'S PALACE ONCE AS AN ACT OF DEFIANCE.

DURING A FRANKEN FAMILY MEETING ABOUT WHETHER AL SHOULD GIVE A SPEECH AT A PRO-WAR RALLY SPONSORED BY CLEAR CHANNEL, EVERYONE EXPRESSED SOME FEAR ABOUT SADDAM HAVING WEAPONS OF MASS DESTRUCTION.

YOU KNOW YOU'RE GOING TO DO THIS, AL. YOU'VE ALREADY MADE UP YOUR MIND.

WHY ARE WE EVEN HAVING THIS MEETING. YOU ALWAYS DO THIS.

DO YOU WANT ME TO SAY YOU SHOULD DO THE SPEECH? FINE. I THINK YOU SHOULD DO THE SPEECH.

THAT WAS ENOUGH FOR AL. OF COURSE, THE FACT THAT AL HAD BEEN THINKING ABOUT DOING A TALK RADIO SHOW AND KNEW THAT CLEAR CHANNEL OWNED OVER 1200 RADIO STATIONS, INCLUDING 247 OF THEM IN THE NATION'S 250 LARGEST RADIO MARKETS DIDN'T HURT, EITHER.

YOU KNOW WHO REALLY HONKS ME OFF? HANS BLIX!

BOOOO!

HANS BLIX SAYS HE CAN'T FIND WEAPONS OF MASS DESTRUCTION IN IRAQ.

WELL, AFTER SADDAM HUSSEIN NUKES THE U.N., IT'S GOING TO BE PRETTY HARD TO FIND HANS BLIX!

OF COURSE, NO ONE WOULD FIND WEAPONS OF MASS DESTRUCTION IN IRAQ AND THAT LEFT AL FEELING VERY ANGRY AT THE BUSH ADMINISTRATION FOR WHAT HE FELT WAS AN ENORMOUS LIE THAT GOT US INVOLVED IN A COSTLY WAR.

HE WAS ALSO ANGRY AT HIMSELF FOR LETTING HIS FEAR LEAD HIM TO SUPPORT A WAR HE HAD NEVER BEEN SURE HE BELIEVED IN.

BUT AL'S ANIMUS TOWARD WHAT HE FELT WERE INCREASINGLY BLATANT RIGHT-WING LIES TOOK REACHED A NEW, PERSONAL LEVEL WHEN HIS FRIEND, SENATOR PAUL WELLSTONE DIED IN A TRAGIC PLANE ACCIDENT.

PAUL WELLSTONE

AL HAS MADE A GOOD LIVING SPEAKING AT CORPORATE EVENTS FOR A FEE. BUT HE NORMALLY SPEAKS FOR OR TO DEMOCRATS FOR FREE. AND THE DEMOCRAT AL DID THE MOST SPEAKING FOR OVER THE YEARS WAS PAUL WELLSTONE.

PART OF IT WAS THAT AS AL GREW UP IN MINNESOTA, WELLSTONE GOT TO KNOW HIS PARENTS.

IN WELLSTONE'S FIRST CAMPAIGN FOR THE SENATE IN 1990 AL'S DAD WAS PART OF A SENIOR CITIZEN THEATER GROUP THAT DID SKITS FOR HIM AT NURSING HOMES.

Wellstone!

THE LAST TIME AL HAD SEEN WELLSTONE WAS LATE SUMMER OF 2002, ABOUT SIX WEEKS BEFORE THE PLANE CRASH THAT WOULD CLAIM HIM.

HOW'S YOUR MOM?

I JUST VISITED HER. IT WAS TOUGH. I COULDN'T EVEN HAVE A CONVERSATION WITH HER.

YOU KNOW, TOUCH MEANS SO MUCH.

THOUGH HE WAS IN THE MIDDLE OF A TOUGH, TIGHT RACE WITH REPUBLICAN CHALLENGER NORM COLEMAN AND WAS FIGHTING FOR HIS POLITICAL LIFE, WELLSTONE'S PRIORITY WHEN TALKING TO AL WAS FIGURING OUT HOW TO HELP AL, WHOSE MOM WAS ILL AND IN A NURSING HOME.

AL TOOK WELLSTONE'S ADVICE, THE KIND A TYPICAL POLITICIAN WOULD NEVER GIVE. TO THIS DAY, HE DOESN'T KNOW IF GREATER EMPHASIS ON "TOUCH" MEANT ANYTHING TO HER, BUT HE KNOWS IT MEANT A LOT TO HIM.

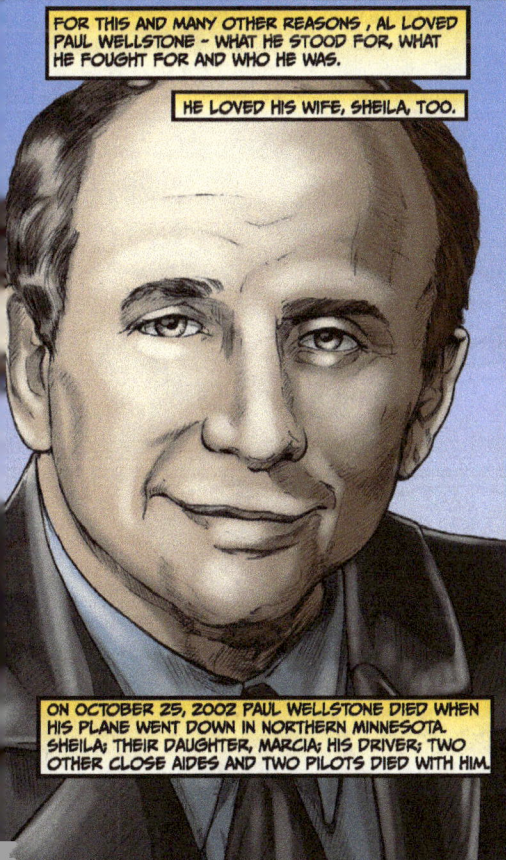

FOR THIS AND MANY OTHER REASONS , AL LOVED PAUL WELLSTONE - WHAT HE STOOD FOR, WHAT HE FOUGHT FOR AND WHO HE WAS.

HE LOVED HIS WIFE, SHEILA, TOO.

FOUR DAYS LATER, A MEMORIAL SERVICE WAS HELD.

RICK KAHN, WELLSTONE'S BEST FRIEND, ENDED A MOVING EULOGY WITH A POLITICAL CALL-TO-ARMS TO FIGHT FOR WHAT WELLSTONE HAD SPENT HIS LIFE FIGHTING FOR.

THEY PULLED A FAST ONE OVER EVERYBODY. THIS WAS NOT A MEMORIAL SERVICE FOR PAUL WELLSTONE.

IT WAS NOT. AND THAT TO ME WHAT'S SO SAD ABOUT IT.

THIS LED TO MANY RIGHT-WING PUNDITS AND POLITICIANS CLAIMING THAT THE MEMORIAL SERVICE HAD BEEN HIJACKED BY PARTISAN ZEALOTS WHO TURNED IT INTO A POLITICAL RALLY.

THIS NARRATIVE ABOUT A "HIJACKED" MEMORIAL MADE IT TO THE MAINSTREAM PRESS.

THE BACKLASH FROM THE PUBLIC HELPED NOT ONLY NORM COLEMAN WIN, BUT RESULTED IN REPUBLICAN GAINS IN THE 2002 ELECTIONS.

AL WAS FURIOUS. HE FELT A BUNCH OF PUNDITS AND OPPORTUNISTIC RIGHT- WING POLITICIANS - MANY OF WHOM HAD NEVER ACTUALLY SEEN THE MEMORIAL, HAD INVENTED A MYTH BASED ON A LIE AND USED THE DEATH OF HIS FRIENDS FOR THEIR OWN PURPOSES.

HE WAS NOT GOING TO LET THEM GET AWAY WITH IT. HE WAS GOING TO EXPOSE THEM.

ON OCTOBER 25, 2002 PAUL WELLSTONE DIED WHEN HIS PLANE WENT DOWN IN NORTHERN MINNESOTA. SHEILA; THEIR DAUGHTER, MARCIA; HIS DRIVER; TWO OTHER CLOSE AIDES AND TWO PILOTS DIED WITH HIM.

YEAH, AL. WHAT CAN I DO FOR YOU?

WELL, FIRST OF ALL, BILL, CONGRATULATIONS ON ALL YOUR SUCCESS.

OKAY. I SAW YOU ON THE OTHER NIGHT ON C-SPAN AND YOU SAID "INSIDE EDITION" HAD WON A COUPLE OF PEABODYS.

THANKS. WHAT'S UP?

THAT'S RIGHT. WE WON TWO.

WELL, MAYBE YOU SHOULD CHECK THAT OUT WITH THE PEABODY PEOPLE, BECAUSE THEY DON'T THINK YOU DID.

THE RIVALRY WITH O'REILLY BEGAN WHEN AL CAUGHT HIM MAKING A CLAIM AL LATER PROVED WASN'T TRUE.

THE RESULT OF AL'S DETERMINATION TO EXPRESS WHAT HE FELT WERE LIES BY EVERYONE FROM RIGHT-WING PUNDITS TO THE BUSH ADMINISTRATION WAS HIS BOOK, "LIES: AND THE LYING LIARS WHO TELL THEM".

WITH FOURTEEN PEOPLE HAVING HELPED TO RESEARCH IT, AL'S TOME WAS A DETAILED, DEVASTATING PIECE OF WORK THAT PLEASED MANY ON THE LEFT.

ALTHOUGH THE BOOK GARNERED HIM FAVORABLE REVIEWS AND NEW FANS, IT ALSO BROUGHT HIM A NEW NEMESIS.

BILL O'REILLY WAS NOT HAPPY.

IT WAS A POLK.

A POLK?

JUST AS PRESTIGIOUS AS A PEABODY.

SO, THERE ARE TWO MOST PRESTIGIOUS AWARDS IN JOURNALISM.

AL, IT'S A VERY PRESTIGIOUS AWARD.

FINE. BUT DON'T YOU THINK IT'S A LITTLE IRONIC THAT YOU GOT IT WRONG ABOUT A JOURNALISM AWARD?

OKAY, AL. GO AFTER ME IF YOU WANT.

AL FELT THAT O'REILLY GETTING SOMETHING WRONG WASN'T A PROBLEM, BUT LATER GOING ON THE ATTACK AND LYING ABOUT IT WAS.

BILL, BILL. THIS IS A PRELIMINARY COVER. I EVEN WANTED THEM TO RETOUCH MY PHOTO. I WANT THEM TO TAKE ABOUT FORTY POUNDS OFF MY ASS.

I DON'T LOOK LIKE THAT! THIS IS WHAT I LOOK LIKE!

BILL, WE'D LOVE TO HAVE A PICTURE OF YOU FROM "THE FACTOR". SOMETHING OF YOU LYING.

ANYTHING WITH YOUR MOUTH OPEN WOULD WORK.

AL RELAYED HIS O'REILLY PEABODY STORY AND OTHER ANECDOTES IN "LIES" TO SEVEN HUNDRED BOOK-SELLERS AND AN AUDIENCE ON C-SPAN.

I'M SORRY I CALL YOU ONE OF THE PEOPLE WHO DO LIE IN MY BOOK, BILL. WELL, I COULD GO ON AND ON -

I KNOW YOU COULD! YOU ALREADY HAVE!

YEAH! YOU TELL 'EM, BILL!

O'REILLY WOULD AGAIN BECOME INCENSED WHEN HE SAW WHAT HE THOUGHT WAS AN UNFLATTERING PHOTO OF HIMSELF ON A BLOWN-UP COVER OF "LIES" AT THE BOOKEXPO AMERICA IN LOS ANGELES, WHERE BOTH OF THEM WOULD SPEAK ABOUT THEIR RESPECTIVE NEW BOOKS.

AL THOUGHT HIS JOKE WOULD LIGHTEN THE MOOD. IT DIDN'T.

MEANWHILE, IT WAS OBVIOUS TO ALL THAT BILL O'REILLY WAS STEWING.

WE'RE SUPPOSED TO BE OUT HERE FOR 15 MINUTES, THIS IDIOT GOES 35. OKAY?

ALL HE'S GOT IN SIX-AND-A-HALF YEARS IS THAT I MISSPOKE, THAT I LABELED A POLK AWARD A PEABODY.

HE WRITES IT IN HIS BOOK. HE TRIES TO MAKE ME OUT TO BE A LIAR.

NONO NONONONO-

NO! I'M NOT GOING TO SHUT UP!

SHUT UP! YOU HAD YOUR 35 MINUTES! SHUT UP!

THIS IS WHAT THIS GUY DOES. THIS IS WHAT HE DOES.

THIS ISN'T YOUR SHOW, BILL! BILL, YOU CAN'T TELL ME -

THIS IS WHAT HE DOES.

TAKE CONTROL, PAT! COME ON!

I THINK I NEED A WHISTLE AND A STRIPED SHIRT. I HAVE TO BE A REFEREE.

MAYBE I WENT ON BECAUSE I GOT SOME LAUGHS, BILL.

YOU DIDN'T MISSPEAK!

WILL YOU PLEASE CONTROL HIM? THIS GUY ACCUSES ME OF BEING A LIAR, LADIES AND GENTLEMEN. ON NATIONAL TELEVISION. BECAUSE I MISSPOKE. IT'S VICIOUS WITH A CAPITAL V.

L FRANKEN

LIES

And the

AFTER REWRITING THE BOOK TO INCLUDE THE BOOKEXPO INCIDENT, FRANKEN SENT IT TO THE PUBLISHER.

HE THEN WENT ON A CELEBRATORY TRIP TO ITALY WHERE HE RECEIVED INCREDIBLE NEWS.

FOX NEWS WAS SUING HIM.

IT WAS AS IF BILL O'REILLY WALKED UP TO YOU AND HANDED YOU A MILLION DOLLARS!

THE CONTROVERSY FROM THE LAWSUIT HAD CAUSED "LIES" TO JUMP FROM NUMBER 489 ON AMAZON, TO NUMBER 12, LITERALLY OVERNIGHT. A FEW HOURS LATER, IT WOULD HIT NUMBER 1.

THE LAWSUIT WAS QUICKLY TOSSED OUT FOR BEING "WHOLLY WITHOUT MERIT" IN THE EYES OF THE COURT.

AL WOULD QUICKLY LEARN THAT MOST OF FOX HAD NOT WANTED TO SUE, BUT BILL O'REILLY HAD INSISTED ON IT.

THE SALES AND BUZZ FROM "LIES" MEANT AL SOON FOUND HIMSELF IN DEMAND TO DEBATE OTHER SUBJECTS OF HIS BOOK, LIKE ANN COULTER.

UH, I WOULD BE HITLER.

HAHA HA HAHAHAHA HA!

A DIFFERENT WAY OF APPROACHING IT WOULD BE, WHO COULD HAVE CHANGED HISTORY IN A VERY IMPORTANT WAY.

ANOTHER POPULAR FAVORITE.

I WOULD WANT TO BE FDR SO THAT I COULD NOT INTRODUCE THE NEW DEAL.

WELL, YOU KNOW, YOU WANT TO CALL OFF THE NEW DEAL. I'D LIKE TO CALL OFF THE HOLOCAUST. YOU KNOW? WORLD WAR II. BUT I'D KEEP THE VOLKSWAGEN.

HIS BOOKS AND HIGH-PROFILE EXCHANGES WITH RIGHT-WING PUNDITS MADE AL INCREASINGLY POPULAR WITH DEMOCRATS.

MY HERO'S HERE.

AS WELL AS HOLLYWOOD.

I'M NOT GOING TO TRY AND BE FUNNY.

I'M NOT GOING TO TRY AND ACT.

IN 2004, AL WOULD START HOSTING "THE AL FRANKEN SHOW", THE LINCHPIN POLITICAL TALK SHOW ON THE NEW AIR AMERICA RADIO, MIXING SERIOUS LEFT-WING POLITICS WITH SKITS.

IN 2007, HE WOULD ANNOUNCE DURING HIS LAST RADIO BROADCAST THAT HE ANNOUNCED HIS CANDIDACY FOR THE U.S. SENATE RACE AGAINST REPUBLICAN NORM COLEMAN, FOR THE SEAT ONCE HELD BY HIS FRIEND PAUL WELLSTONE.

HE JUST MAKES STUFF UP AND THEN WHEN HE GETS BACKED INTO A CORNER, HE MAKES MORE STUFF UP.

IT'S AMAZING! IT'S HILARIOUS! I LOVE BILL O'REILLY.

THE RACE WAS VERY CLOSE AND GOT HEATED AT TIMES.

YOU CAN TAKE THIS GUY! YOU CAN TAKE HIM!

IT ALSO GOT A BIT NASTY, AS WHEN THE COLEMAN CAMPAIGN RAN AN AD THAT TRIED TO PORTRAY AL AS ANGRY.

TURNS OUT HE ACTUALLY WAS IMITATING PAUL WELLSTONE CHEERING HIS SON DAVID ON DURING A CROSS-COUNTRY RACE.

ELECTING UNQUALIFIED PEOPLE SIMPLY BECAUSE YOU ARE ANGRY WITH THE BUSH ADMINISTRATION WILL DRASTICALLY WEAKEN THIS COUNTRY. THE BEST EXAMPLE I CAN GIVE YOU IS AL FRANKEN, WHO IS RUNNING FOR THE SENATE IN MINNESOTA.

A FAR-LEFT EXTREMIST, FRANKEN'S TENURE ON THE AIR AMERICA RADIO NETWORK WAS PUNCTUATED BY ONE WORD: HATE. THE MAN IS A SMEAR MERCHANT AND A RANK LIAR, UNQUALIFIED FOR ANY ELECTED OFFICE.

ELECTION DAY ENDED WITH COLEMAN AHEAD BY 200 VOTES. HOWEVER, A MANDATORY RECOUNT DUE TO THE CLOSE MARGIN GAVE AL THE LEAD BY 300 VOTES.

AS COLEMAN'S LEAD SHRANK AND THEN DISAPPEARED, CONSERVATIVE COMMENTATORS VOICED INCREASING SUSPICION AND ANGER.

INCLUDING BILL O' REILLY...

SEAN HANNITY ...

I WANT AL FRANKEN TO SUE ME.

BECAUSE FOR HIM TO CHALLENGE THESE BALLOTS WHICH ARE SO CLEARLY FOR NORM COLEMAN, I THINK IT SHOWS HE'S TRYING TO STEAL THE ELECTION.

SEAN HANNITY

LAURA INGRAHAM...

THIS IS VOTE-COUNTING BY DAVID COPPERFIELD. I MEAN, THIS IS LIKE A DAVID BLAINE ILLUSIONIST FINDING VOTES EVERYWHERE.

THIS IS MY RULE OF THUMB. ANY TIME A REPUBLICAN IN A RACE LIKE THIS IS ONLY WINNING BY A THOUSAND VOTES OR LESS, THEN YOU CAN BET THAT THAT REPUBLICAN'S GONNA END UP LOSING THAT SEAT.

DICK MORRIS.

I THINK THERE'S FUNNY BUSINESS GOING ON. THERE'S NO QUESTION THAT THERE'S CHEATING GOING ON.

THERE'S A COUNTY WHERE THERE'S 177 MORE VOTES THAN THERE ARE VOTERS.

THIS IS OUTRIGHT LARCENY. A TOTAL THEFT.

DICK MORRIS

COLEMAN LOST EVERY APPEAL.

TYPICALLY, THE JUDGES ASK QUESTIONS.

I SEE THAT YOU ARE NOT BUYING THIS, JUDGE REILLY?

I THOUGHT I HAD A POKER FACE.

MY CONCERN IS THAT THE LEGISLATURE PASSED A STATUTE, THAT I TOOK AN OATH TO UPHOLD THE LAW.

NOPE. I DON'T THINK SO. BUT IN ANY EVENT, WHAT CAN I TELL YOU THAT WILL HELP YOU TO BUY IT?

YOUR CONCERN IS THAT THERE'S A NEED FOR AN APPLICATION, GRANTED –

RIGHT, AND HOW ARE YOU NOT UPHOLDING THE LAW, MAY I ASK –

WHILE SOME FOUND IT UNSEEMLY THAT A JUDGE THAT WOULD HELP DECIDE THE CASE WAS GIGGLING LIKE A SCHOOLGIRL IN THE COURTROOM, THE FACT REMAINS COLEMAN LOST EVERY SINGLE APPEAL.

WHEN THE MINNESOTA SUPREME COURT RULED AGAINST HIM, COLEMAN DECIDED NOT TO APPEAL TO THE U.S. SUPREME COURT.

EIGHT MONTHS AFTER ELECTION DAY, HE CONCEDED.

I JUST HAD A CONVERSATION WITH AL FRANKEN CONGRATULATING HIM ON HIS VICTORY...

...AND I TOLD HIM IT'S THE BEST JOB THAT HE'LL EVER HAVE, REPRESENTING THE PEOPLE OF MINNESOTA.

I RECEIVED A VERY GRACIOUS CALL FROM SENATOR COLEMAN A LITTLE WHILE AGO. HE WISHED ME WELL.

I WISHED HIM WELL AND WE AGREED THAT IT IS TIME TO BRING THIS STATE TOGETHER.

SO THE CITIZENS OF THE STATE OF MINNESOTA HAVE ELECTED AL FRANKEN TO REPRESENT THEM AS THEIR SENATOR IN WASHINGTON, D.C.

SOME SAY HE IS A VICIOUS, PETTY MAN UNWORTHY OF THE OFFICE.

OTHERS SAY HE FIGHTS FOR THE LITTLE GUY AND TAKES ON THE POWERFUL WITH PASSION, WIT AND HUMOR.

WHATEVER YOUR OPINION OF THE MAN, ONE THING IS CERTAIN.

THE PEOPLE FROM "THE LAND OF 1000 LAKES" HAVE ELECTED SOMEONE WHO IS TRULY ONE OF A KIND.

# BARACK OBAMA

# BARACK OBAMA

IT'S HARD TO PINPOINT JUST WHEN AMERICA STARTED VIEWING *BARACK OBAMA* AS AN IDEALIZED *SUPERMAN*... MYTHOLOGIZED EVEN AS HE *LIVES* AND *BREATHES*.

AFTER ALL, IN WHAT BIZARRO VERSION OF AMERICA DOES THE MAINSTREAM SO QUICKLY AND EFFORTLESSLY LATCH ONTO A POLITICAL FIGURE AS A SUPERHERO, AFTER BEING LET DOWN *AGAIN* AND *AGAIN* BY THEM?

THIS SPOKE TO SOMETHING *DEEP*-- I'M NOT EVEN SURE KENNEDY GOT A BOBBLEHEAD IN HIS DAY.

BUT, IMPROBABLY, IT *REALLY* HAPPENED.

FASTER THAN A SPEEDING BULLET, A SELF-PROCLAIMED *'SKINNY GUY WITH A FUNNY NAME'* ARRIVED AND FLIPPED WASHINGTON ON ITS EAR.

BECAUSE OF THIS, YOU'LL NOW HAVE A DIFFICULT TIME EXPLAINING TO YOUR KIDS HOW *EXTRAORDINARY* IT WAS THAT A BLACK MAN BECAME THE 44TH *PRESIDENT* OF THE UNITED STATES.

TO *FUTURE* GENERATIONS, THIS MINOR TIDBIT WILL *NOT* SEEM STRANGE *AT ALL*.

EVERY STORY HAS A BEGINNING BUT, FOR *THIS* AUTHOR'S TWO CENTS, BARACK OBAMA'S STORY HAS A PRETTY *UNUSUAL* ONE...

SO, ANYWAY... I SUPPOSE YOU'RE WONDERING WHAT THIS ALL HAS TO DO WITH BARACK OBAMA. YOU KNOW, BESIDES THAT HE MUST HAVE EATEN HIS SHARE OF HORSESHOES WHILE HANGING OUT IN SPRINGFIELD. *HEY*, THE GUY USED TO *CHAIN SMOKE*, SO WHAT'S ONE MORE *AWFUL HABIT?*

...WHAT I THINK IT MEANS, IS THAT UNTIL *BARACK OBAMA* WALKED ON STAGE TO DELIVER THE DEMOCRATIC NATIONAL CONVENTION KEYNOTE SPEECH IN *2004*, THE WHOLE OF AMERICAN POLITICS SEEMED ABOUT AS APPETIZING AS A GREASY, STOMACH-CHURNING, HAMBURGER-INDUCED BELLY CRAMP (WITH FRIES ON TOP). BUT WHEN HE TOLD HIS STORY...

ON BEHALF OF THE GREAT STATE OF ILLINOIS, CROSSROADS OF A NATION, LAND OF *LINCOLN*, LET ME EXPRESS MY *DEEP* GRATITUDE FOR THE PRIVILEGE OF ADDRESSING THIS CONVENTION.

TONIGHT IS A PARTICULAR HONOR FOR ME BECAUSE, LET'S FACE IT, MY PRESENCE ON THIS STAGE IS PRETTY UNLIKELY.

MY FATHER WAS A FOREIGN STUDENT, BORN AND RAISED IN A SMALL VILLAGE IN *KENYA*. HE GREW UP HERDING GOATS, WENT TO SCHOOL IN A TIN-ROOF SHACK...

...HE SEEMED TO SPELL *R-E-L-I-E-F* FOR A LOT OF PEOPLE FED UP WITH THE JUNK BEING FED TO THEM, WHO WERE HUNGRY FOR SOMETHING BETTER. SUDDENLY, THE NATION HAD FOUND ITS POLITICAL APPETITE AGAIN.

BUT MAYBE I'M GETTING AHEAD OF THINGS. PEOPLE DON'T START WAVING SIGNS AROUND WITH YOUR *NAME* ON IT OVERNIGHT.

OR NAMING *LOGS* AFTER YOU!

UMM... *YEAH.* YOU SAID IT, ABE.

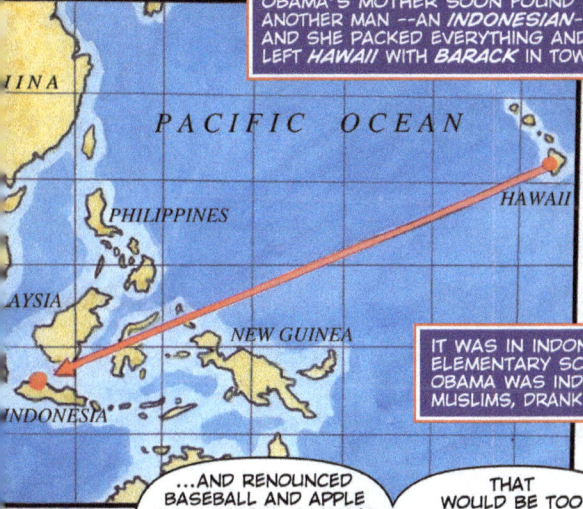

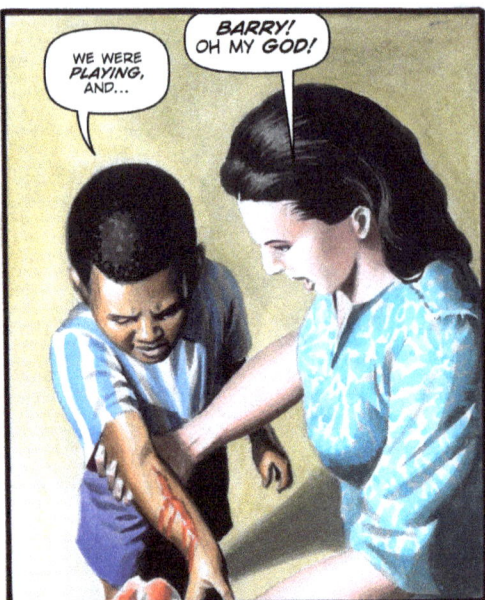

**Panel 1:** I GUESS A SMALL TOWN MAYOR IS SORT OF LIKE A COMMUNITY *ORGANIZER*, EXCEPT THAT YOU HAVE ACTUAL RESPONSIBILITIES.

HAHAHAHA

HE PLAYED IT COOL, BUT SARAH PALIN'S FAMOUS DIG, REPEATED AT EVERY CAMPAIGN STOP, HAD TO STING OBAMA. MAYBE IT PROMPTED HIS SLY "LIPSTICK ON A PIG" JOKE. BOTH SIDES GOT THEIR SHOTS IN.

**Panel 2:** BUT AS AN ORGANIZER, HE TOOK A NEIGHBORHOOD FROM NOTHING TO SECURING A BUDGET OF $400,000 FOR JOB PLACEMENT PROGRAMS AND HOUSING REFORM. AFTER GRADUATING HARVARD AS A TOP LAWYER, THE 30-YEAR-OLD UPSTART MADE GOOD ON HIS PROMISE TO RETURN TO THE SOUTH SIDE AND FOUGHT FOR ECONOMIC DEVELOPMENT AND CIVIL RIGHTS.

HE TURNED DOWN SOME BIG *JOB OFFERS* TO DO IT.

SO I'M NOT SURE HOW YOU'D DEFINE "ACTUAL *RESPONSIBILITIES*," BUT I THINK HE HAD 'EM IN SPADES.

**Panel 3:** OBAMA'S MASSIVELY ORGANIZED "ILLINOIS PROJECT VOTE" BROUGHT IN *150,000* NEW BLACK VOTERS. ALL IN ALL, AFRICAN AMERICANS TURNED OUT *600,000* STRONG FOR THE *1993* PRESIDENTIAL ELECTION, TURNING ILLINOIS DEMOCRATIC FOR THE FIRST TIME SINCE *1964*, WHEN BARACK WAS THREE.

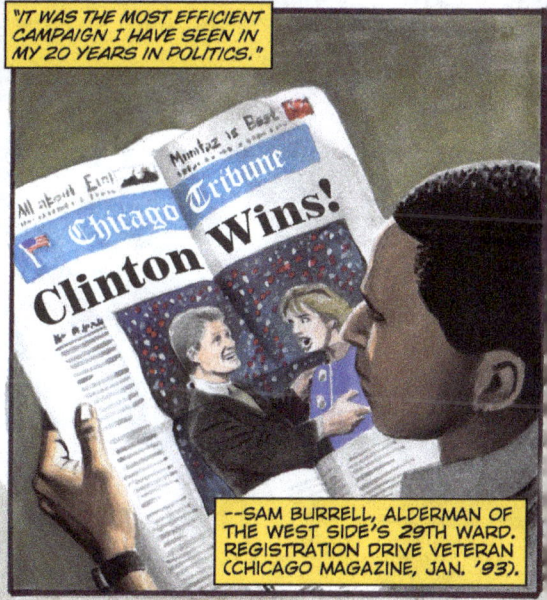

POWER! X

REGISTER TO VOTE HERE
Project VOTE
103 FM

It's a POWER thing! X
VOTE THRS. NOV. 2

**Panel 4:** *"IT WAS THE MOST EFFICIENT CAMPAIGN I HAVE SEEN IN MY 20 YEARS IN POLITICS."*

Chicago Tribune

Clinton Wins!

--SAM BURRELL, ALDERMAN OF THE WEST SIDE'S *29TH* WARD, REGISTRATION DRIVE VETERAN (CHICAGO MAGAZINE, JAN. *'93*).

**Panel 5:** AND NOW, IT MADE SENSE TO TRY AND GET MORE DONE...

...BY RUNNING FOR STATE SENATE? IN ILLINOIS? YOU KNOW HOW *DIRTY* ILLINOIS POLITICS ARE, RIGHT? JUST WHAT DO YOU THINK YOU'RE GOING TO ACCOMPLISH?

WELL, I... I GUESS WE'LL SEE.

ILLINOIS POLITICS HAVE... A *REPUTATION*. THERE'S A REASON OUR MOTTO IS "ILLINOIS: WHERE THE GOVERNORS MAKE THE LICENSE PLATES."

WE'VE HAD SEVEN GOVERNORS INDICTED OR ARRESTED-- AND *THOSE* WERE JUST THE GUYS STUPID ENOUGH TO GET *CAUGHT*.

YOU'VE PROBABLY HEARD OF *ROD BLAGOJEVICH*, WHO ALLEGEDLY TRIED TO SELL OBAMA'S VACANT SENATE SEAT AND GOT IMPEACHED.

OOOO! OOOO! I WANT A COMIC BOOK!

MAKE ONE ABOUT *ME*!

PUT *ME* IN A COMIC BOOK!

HERE'S A TRUE STORY. I'M WALKING THROUGH SPRINGFIELD'S ABRAHAM LINCOLN PRESIDENTIAL MUSEUM AND I SPOT A PENNY ON THE GROUND...

I ALMOST WALK RIGHT INTO THIS OLD GUY. I LOOK UP TO APOLOGIZE...

...AND I'M NOSE TO NOSE WITH EX-GOVERNOR GEORGE RYAN: THE GUY NOW IN PRISON FOR A *"LICENSES-FOR-BRIBES"* SCANDAL. A TRUCK DRIVER WHO OBTAINED ONE OF THESE LICENSES GOT IN A WRECK THAT KILLED *SIX LITTLE KIDS*, WHICH KICKED OFF THE INVESTIGATION. IT WAS *ALL OVER* THE NEWS.

AND HERE HE WAS. THIS *75-YEAR-OLD RACKETEER*, EXTORTIONIST, ELECTED FELON... JUST STROLLING AROUND IN MY TOWN. STANDING IN *LINCOLN'S SHADOW*. THE *AUDACITY*.

TIME AND AGAIN, MEN LIKE GEORGE RYAN *SHAPED* MY CYNICAL VIEW OF POLITICS.

IN THE STATE SENATE, OBAMA ONCE WORKED ACROSS PARTY LINES WITH RYAN TO OVERHAUL THE STATE'S DEATH PENALTY SYSTEM, FIGHT PREDATORY HOUSING LENDERS AND GIVE TAX BREAKS TO THE POOR. AND, SOMEHOW, HE AVOIDED THE *TEMPTATIONS* OF ABUSING POWER AND THE *"SMALLNESS OF POLITICS."*

THIS DIDN'T MAKE AS MUCH NEWS.

MOST STILL HADN'T HEARD OF *OBAMA* IN *2004*: THOUGH HE HAD WRITTEN TWO BEST-SELLING BOOKS, RAN AND LOST FOR US SENATOR ONCE, EVENTUALLY BECAME A US SENATOR AND SIMPLY STUCK OUT LIKE A SORE THUMB ON THE POLITICAL SCENE.

BARACK OBAMA
The *AUDACITY* of HOPE

WHAT'S *CRAZY* IS THAT OBAMA'S EARLY BUZZ GOT AROUND THE SAME WAY THE "KITTEN PLAYING PIANO" DID: *VIRAL VIDEO*. THIS WAS A FIRST.

WE COACH LITTLE LEAGUE IN THE *BLUE* STATES, AND, YES, WE'VE GOT SOME *GAY* FRIENDS IN THE *RED* STATES... WE ARE ALL ONE PEOPLE...

IN OBAMA'S EVENTUAL ARSENAL OF ARTICULATE, ELOQUENT SPEECHES, THE '04 *DNC ADDRESS* WOULD BE OBAMA'S '*FREEBIRD*'... HE WOVE IT INTO HIS STUMP SPEECHES LATER (AD NAUSEUM, AT TIMES) LIKE A GREATEST HIT TRACK.

THERE IS NOT A *LIBERAL* AMERICA AND A *CONSERVATIVE* AMERICA; THERE IS THE *UNITED STATES OF AMERICA!*

I'M NOT TALKING ABOUT BLIND OPTIMISM HERE, THE ALMOST WILLFUL IGNORANCE THAT THINKS UNEMPLOYMENT WILL GO *AWAY* IF WE JUST DON'T THINK ABOUT IT, OR THE HEALTH-CARE CRISIS WILL SOLVE ITSELF IF WE JUST *IGNORE* IT.

THAT'S NOT WHAT I'M TALKING ABOUT. I'M *TALKING* ABOUT SOMETHING MORE SUBSTANTIAL...

*HOPE*. HOPE IN THE FACE OF DIFFICULTY, HOPE IN THE FACE OF UNCERTAINTY, THE AUDACITY OF HOPE! IN THE END, THAT IS GOD'S GREATEST GIFT TO US, THE BEDROCK OF THIS NATION, A BELIEF IN THINGS NOT SEEN, A BELIEF THAT THERE ARE BETTER DAYS AHEAD...

"OHIO DISPUTED..."

"TOO CLOSE TO CALL..."

"SWIFT BOAT"

"FLIP FLOP"

"VOTING CONTROVERSY"

"DIEBOLD MACHINES"

"BUSH WINS SECOND TERM"

"BALLOT RE-COUNT"

"KERRY CAMP PULLS OUT"

"FOUR MORE YEARS"

"NO CLEAR WINNER AT THIS HOUR..."

"STATES CONTESTED"

BUT THE *2004 ELECTION* WASN'T SOMETHING YOU'D CALL "OPTIMISTIC." THIS WAS DIRTY BUSINESS.

BUT DESPITE PEOPLE'S DOUBTS AND DISBELIEF, OBAMA'S REAL OBSTACLE COULD BE SUMMED UP IN ONE WORD:

HILLARY.

HEADSTRONG. INTELLIGENT. DETERMINED. CLAWED HER WAY THOUGH THE POLITICAL MUD --AND HER HUSBAND'S MISGIVINGS-- TO BECOME THE FIRST SERIOUS WOMAN CANDIDATE FOR PRESIDENT. NOW THIS WAS GOING TO BE EXCITING.

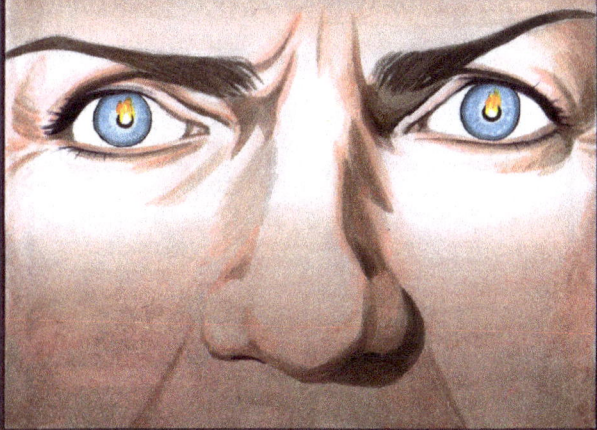

TO COUNTER, GUYS LIKE *DAVID PLOUFFE*, HIS CAMPAIGN MANAGER, MIXED OBAMA'S OLD SCHOOL METHODS --GRASSROOTS ORGANIZING-- WITH THE UNTAPPED NEW SCHOOL...

THEY'VE UNDERESTIMATED THE WEB... OUR SMALL ONLINE *DONATIONS* NUMBER IN THE HUNDREDS OF *THOUSANDS*, WE'RE MOBILIZING SUPPORTERS NATIONWIDE THROUGH BLOGGING AND TEXT MESSAGES... I'M *TELLING* YOU, *THIS* IS HOW WE DO IT.

IT WAS EFFECTIVE. I STILL CAN'T GET OFF THEIR EMAIL CHAIN-- MY FREAKING *MOM* EMAILS ME LESS THAN DAVID PLOUFFE.

IN THE FIRST REAL TEST --THE *2007* IOWA CAUCUS-- VOTERS SHOCKED PUNDITS BY PICKING OBAMA OVER HILARY CLINTON AND JOHN EDWARDS. THE MAJORITY VOTERS WERE FIRST TIME CACAUSGOERS.

...I'LL NEVER FORGET THAT MY JOURNEY BEGAN ON THE STREETS OF CHICAGO DOING WHAT SO MANY OF YOU HAVE DONE FOR *THIS* CAMPAIGN AND *ALL* THE CAMPAIGNS HERE IN IOWA-- ORGANIZING, AND WORKING, AND FIGHTING TO MAKE PEOPLE'S LIVES JUST A LITTLE BIT BETTER.

...IN THIS ELECTION, WE ARE READY TO BELIEVE AGAIN. THANK YOU, IOWA.

THE GUY'S A *ROCK STAR!* PEOPLE *LOVE* IT!

AND THE *MEDIA* WERE EATING IT UP LIKE IT WAS COVERED IN SPICY CHEESE SAUCE.

HARDBALL

AMERICANS ARE *SKEPTICAL* OF THIS *"ROCK STAR"* BALONEY!

FOX NEWS channel

AND THEN, *REV. JEREMIAH WRIGHT* SHOWED UP.

HI-YA, AND GOD $#%*, AMERICA!

I MEAN... GOD BLESS AMERICA.

NOBODY'S *FILMING THIS*, RIGHT?

OBAMA'S CHICAGO PASTOR AND FRIEND SAID SOME PRETTY INFLAMMATORY STUFF ABOUT RACE AND AMERICA IN HIS SERMONS. IN CONTEXT OR NOT, IT WAS A PROBLEM FOR THE CAMPAIGN...

1960S, TEXAS: OBAMA'S GRANDMA TOOT IS SCREAMED AT BY A COLLEAGUE FOR SIMPLY ADDRESSING A BLACK CO-WORKER, A WWII VET-TURNED-JANITOR, AS 'MISTER.' THE COLLEAGUE THEN SPOUTED OFF A LIST OF UGLY SLURS ABOUT THE MAN, WHICH HE OVERHEARD ENTIRELY.

TELL ME... WHAT HAVE WE EVER DONE TO BE *TREATED* SO *MEAN?*

FROM THAT DAY ON, *TOOT* CONTINUED ADDRESSING HIM AS *'MISTER* REED,' DESPITE HER CO-WORKERS GLARES.

BUT EVEN THIS COMPASSIONATE GRANDMOTHER WAS NOT IMMUNE TO THE COMPLICATIONS OF RACE RELATIONS. OBAMA KNEW THIS. THESE GRAY ISSUES *DEFINED* HIM. SO HE CHOSE FRANK DISCUSSION, NOT PR SPIN, TO HANDLE HIS REV. WRIGHT PROBLEM...

I CAN NO MORE DISOWN [REV. WRIGHT] THAN I CAN DISOWN MY WHITE GRANDMOTHER... A WOMAN WHO SACRIFICED AGAIN AND AGAIN FOR ME, A WOMAN WHO LOVES ME AS MUCH AS SHE LOVES ANYTHING IN THIS WORLD, BUT A WOMAN WHO ONCE CONFESSED HER FEAR OF BLACK MEN WHO PASSED HER BY ON THE STREET, AND WHO ON MORE THAN ONE OCCASION HAS UTTERED RACIAL OR ETHNIC STEREOTYPES THAT MADE ME *CRINGE.*

THESE PEOPLE ARE A PART OF ME. AND THEY ARE PART OF *AMERICA,* THIS COUNTRY I LOVE.

WE HAVE A CHOICE IN THIS COUNTRY... WE CAN TACKLE RACE ONLY AS SPECTACLE --AS WE DID IN THE OJ TRIAL-- OR IN THE WAKE OF TRAGEDY --AS WE DID IN THE AFTERMATH OF KATRINA-- OR AS FODDER FOR THE NIGHTLY NEWS...

...OR AT THIS MOMENT, IN THIS ELECTION, WE CAN COME TOGETHER AND SAY, 'NOT THIS TIME.'

THIS UNION MAY NEVER BE PERFECT, BUT GENERATION AFTER GENERATION HAS SHOWN THAT IT CAN ALWAYS BE PERFECTED.

McCAIN'S STORY IS ONE FOR *ANOTHER* COMIC BOOK, BUT HERE ARE THE BASICS.

WAR HERO AND P.O.W.

CATCH PHRASE: "DRILL, BABY, DRILL!"

WENT FROM DEAD LAST (WITH NO CAMPAIGN MONEY) TO UNDERDOG CHAMPION OF '08 REPUBLICAN PRIMARIES

73 YEARS YOUNG

STRONGLY COMMITTED TO WAR IN IRAQ CURING CAMPAIGN

DRIVES A TRICKED OUT BUS CALLED THE "STRAIGHT TALK EXPRESS"

SAYS "PORK BARREL" A LOT

BUSH SMEAR ADS DERAILED HIS 2000 PRESIDENTIAL BID

...ALSO, HIS "MAVERICK" REPUTATION RUBBED THE REPUBLICAN BASE THE WRONG WAY. HE WAS THE LAST NOMINEE THEY WANTED. BUT, THEN AGAIN, WHO KNOWS *WHAT* THE GOP WANTED.

EARLY ON, THEIR MESSAGE BOILED DOWN TO "WE'RE NOT GEORGE W. BUSH-- VOTE FOR US."

McCAIN WASTED NO TIME HAMMERING ON OBAMA'S FOREIGN POLICY INEXPERIENCE, TREATING HIM AS *NAIVE*.

IT WOULD BE A WONDERFUL THING IF WE LIVED IN A WORLD WHERE WE DON'T HAVE ENEMIES. THAT'S NOT THE WORLD WE LIVE IN.

AND UNTIL SEN. OBAMA UNDERSTANDS THAT REALITY, THE AMERICAN PEOPLE HAVE EVERY REASON TO DOUBT WHETHER HE HAS STRENGTH, JUDGMENT AND DETERMINATION TO KEEP US SAFE.

McCAIN
JOHNMCCAIN.C

IT'S TRUE THAT *OBAMA* HAD DIFFERENT IDEAS ABOUT HOW TO APPROACH FOREIGN RELATIONS.

APRIL, 2007

YOU KNOW THAT OLD *BEACH BOYS* SONG? "BOMB IRAN?" BOMB, BOMB, BOMB... BOMB, BOMB IRAN...

HEH, HEH...

CLEARLY MEANT TO EVOKE KENNEDY, OBAMA SPOKE TO A CROWD OF 200,000 IN BERLIN, AND THEN MET WITH LEADERS IN IRAQ, AFGHANISTAN, FRANCE AND ENGLAND TO BUMP UP HIS FOREIGN CRED. TO MCCAIN'S CHAGRIN, HE WAS A HIT.

JA KÖNNEN WIR!

TRANSLATION: "YES WE CAN!"... I THINK. I DON'T SPEAK GERMAN.

BUT HE STILL HAD PLENTY OF WORK TO DO RIGHT HERE AT HOME, CONVINCING "RED STATES" HE WASN'T AN "ARUGLA EATIN' ELITIST."

...SO IT'S NOT SURPRISING THAT THEY GET BITTER, THEY CLING TO GUNS OR RELIGION OR ANTIPATHY TO PEOPLE WHO AREN'T LIKE THEM.

I LIKE JOHN MCCAIN. I REALLY DO. BUT THE CLOSER IT GOT TO ELECTION DAY, THE MORE IT SEEMED LIKE HE WAS GETTING DESPERATE. AND MCCAIN'S DESPERATION WORE TWO FACES...

ENTER "HOCKEY MOM" SARAH PALIN, HIS SURPRISE VICE PRESIDENTIAL PICK, AND JOE THE PLUMBER.

IN CASE
EMERGENC

BREAK GLAS

HI-YA! YOU BETCHA! DARN TOOTIN'! SHUCKY DANG DERN!

WHILE THESE FASCINATING AND STRANGE POLITICAL FIGURES TOOK THE FOCUS OFF OBAMA AS INTENDED, MCCAIN NEVER QUITE WRESTLED THE ATTENTION BACK FROM THEM...

OBAMA'S VP PICK, SENIOR SENATOR *JOE BIDEN*, SEEMED TO HANDLE HER OK. THE WHOLE THING WAS SURREAL. AND VERY ENTERTAINING.

HOW LONG HAVE I BEEN AT THIS, LIKE FIVE WEEKS? SO THERE HASN'T BEEN A WHOLE LOT THAT I'VE PROMISED, EXCEPT TO DO WHAT IS RIGHT FOR THE AMERICAN PEOPLE...

IS SHE FOR *REAL*?

AND THAT FINAL PRESIDENTIAL DEBATE? *YEESH*. 10 YEARS LATER, HERE'S WHAT WE'LL *REMEMBER*...

JOE THE PLUMBER. JOE THE PLUMBER! JOE THE PLUMBER, MY FRIENDS!

JOE THE PLUMBER? JOE THE PLUMBER. FOLKS, *UMMMM*... LET ME BE CLEAR: JOE THE PLUMBER.

...MCCAIN'S AMERICAN *"EVERYMAN"* WAS MENTIONED *26* TIMES.

BUT MARKETS NOSE DIVED AND CHANGED THE DEBATE FROM IRAQ TO WALL STREET OVERNIGHT.

BY THE TIME YOU READ THIS, I HOPE THE ECONOMY ISN'T STILL IN THE WORST SHAPE IT'S BEEN SINCE THE DEPRESSION. IF IT IS... UMM, PLEASE BUY THIS COMIC BOOK ANYWAY. I'M STARVING.

MCCAIN'S CAMP POUNCED ON AN OBAMA QUOTE, TURNING IT INTO A LAST MINUTE SCARE PHRASE...

...TIME TO SPREAD THE WEALTH AROUND.

SOCIALIST *SCUM*!

THE *FUNDAMENTALS* OF OUR ECONOMY ARE STRONG!

AND *OBAMA'S TEAM* POUNCED RIGHT BACK...

WHAT I *MEANT* WAS...

CRAP.

AT THE 11TH HOUR, MCCAIN AND PALIN ACCUSED OBAMA OF "PALLING AROUND WITH TERRORISTS," BECAUSE OF A CHANCE MEETING WITH EX-HIPPIE WAR ACTIVIST *WILLIAM AYERS*. MORE DISTRACTIONS.

I DON'T *BUY* THE IDEA THAT GUILT BY ASSOCIATION SHOULD BE ANY PART OF OUR *POLITICS*, AND THE INTERESTING THING IS AS MUCH AS THIS WAS CREATED AS AN ISSUE IN THE CAMPAIGN, IT APPEARS FOR MOST PEOPLE IT HAD NO TRACTION. IT HAD *NO MEANING*.

Bill Ayers **ABC News, Nov. 2008**

BUT NOW IT WAS PENCILS DOWN TIME, CLASS:

NOV. 4, 2008.

*ELECTION DAY.*

THERE WOULD BE NO RE-COUNT, NO HANGING CHADS. "THE AMERICAN PEOPLE HAVE SPOKEN, AND THEY HAVE SPOKEN CLEARLY," McCAIN SAID, GRACIOUSLY, IN HIS CONCESSION SPEECH.

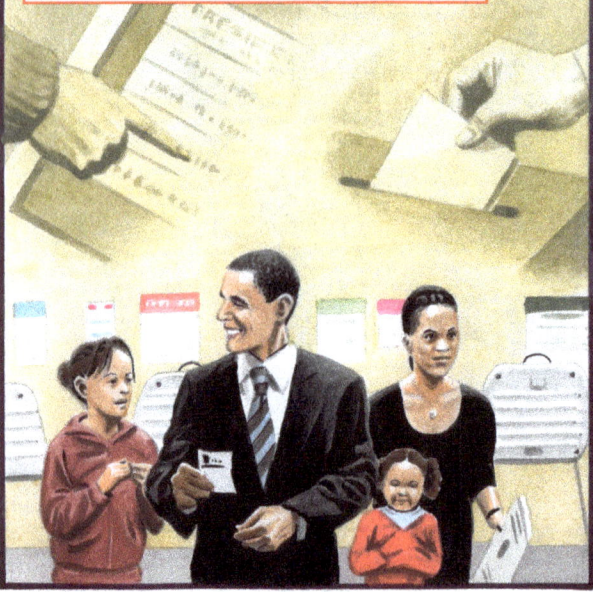

...OBAMA'S GRANDMOTHER *TOOT*, WHO HELPED SHAPE HER GRANDSON'S *UNLIKELY* UPBRINGING, CAST HER VOTE BUT WOULDN'T HEAR THE RESULTS. STILL, SHE *MUST* HAVE KNOWN.

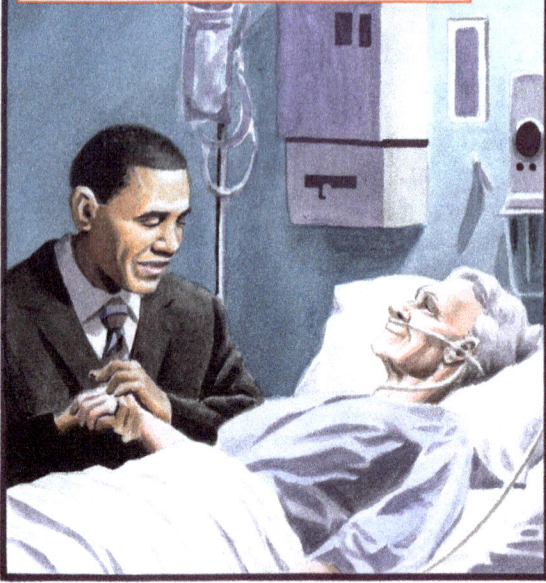

SLAVES WHO BUILT THE WHITE HOUSE OBAMA WOULD ONE DAY TAKE OATH TO SERVE IN... THEY *MUST* HAVE HOPED.

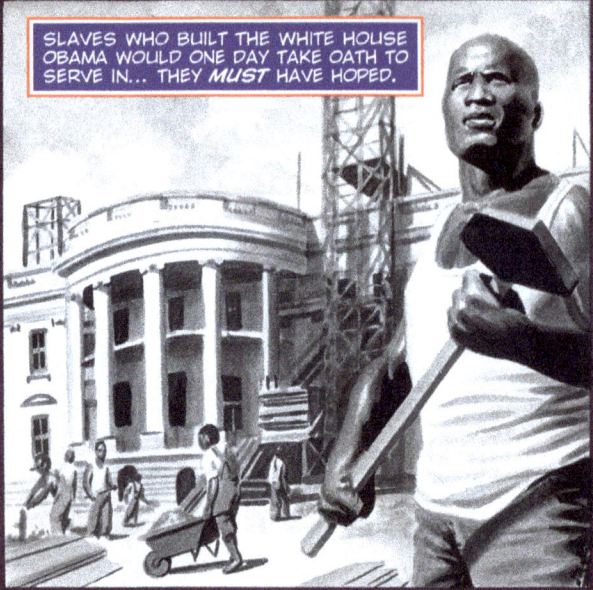

ANN NIXON COOPER, WHO WOULD TURN *106* BEFORE SHE SAW THIS DAY... SHE *MUST* HAVE DREAMED...

BARACK'S PARENTS. THEY TOOK THAT INCREDIBLE CHANCE YEARS AGO...

BUT...

JUST ONE DATE. COME ON, WHAT COULD HAPPEN?

HE HAD TO HAVE FELT THE *WEIGHT*. THE *HISTORY*. IT MUST HAVE BEEN *OVERWHELMING*.

# BLUEWATER
## COMICS

**Darren G. Davis**
Publisher

**Jason Schultz**
Vice President

**Jackie Stickley**
New Business Development

**Jarred Weisfeld**
Literary Manager

**Kailey Marsh**
Entertainment Manager

**Warren Montgomery**
Coordinator

**Nikki Borror**
Coordinator

**Maggie Jessup**
Publicity

# BLUEWATER
## COMICS

## www.bluewaterprod.com

www.ingramcontent.com/pod-product-compliance
Lightning Source LLC
Chambersburg PA
CBHW062050090426
42740CB00016B/3083